REBIRTH

FROM HEARTBREAK TO HAPPINESS

by

Mark Holmes

MARK HOLMES

Copyright © 2019 Mark Holmes

All rights reserved.

ISBN: 978-1-6929-4671-5
Cover photograph : Mark Holmes on his Triumph Rocket X at sunset, Uluru, Northern Territory, Australia.

For Sue

CONTENTS

1	Eleven days.	1
2	Knock, knock.	9
3	*Vai, Vivi e Ritorno.*	25
4	Bosphorus and bullets.	32
5	Lord Ganesha.	49
6	Love, loss, and love again.	66
7	*"Jum, jum"* to the top of the world.	71
8	Hop, skip and jump through Asia.	78
9	Time to reflect with some very good lemonade.	89
10	I exist.	97
11	Crazy little thing called love.	98
12	The tyranny of distance.	102
13	Friends, old and new.	114
14	Gormless Llamas.	120
15	Thongs and other things.	129

16	No money for a teacher.	146
17	I love you more than tacos.	158
18	Life in the high Andes.	168
19	Lost in Lima.	177
20	Fertility bottoms.	189
21	Trump(ed).	194
22	Fixed.	205
	Addedndum	217

1. Eleven days.

I'm staring out of the window into light drizzle today. The grey clouds are flattened by grey mist, while clinging to grey buildings. All the shades are from the same palette. The colour that I am used to seeing is simply not there. I've had many colourless days recently. My eyes have glazed over too, further obscuring my vision.

The view of London from my apartment is often like this in winter, but more usually it is spectacular. A change of season, the weather, and the time of day, frequently alters the vista, sometimes substantially. Shafts of light can hit a building, illuminating a familiar landmark with an unfamiliar golden glow. From time to time the setting sun behind me has an unnerving habit of appearing to insert itself into glazed buildings, and produces a fierce orange-red fiery light as if lit from within. At night the city sparkles with millions of coloured lights, and later diminishes towards dawn. The river below me reflects some of that glory and sometimes fills with laughter from revellers on a party boat. At other times barges pass downstream, full of our rubbish.

Today is a rubbish day. The telephone rings and I answer to a voice that has become familiar to me in recent weeks. I listen while he explains the reason for his call this time. I am not saying much in return but interrupt to ask "Are you saying that is it now? Am I needed for anything else?".

The caller said there might be some more questions in due course, perhaps from others involved in the procedures. The answer to my questions was qualified, but basically it was, "No". So that was how it ended.

I returned to staring out of the window again. I don't quite remember but I think I might have been pacing slowly around the room during the call. I arrived at a tall book cabinet beside the window, folded my arms, and slumped against it. The company that my wife and I had run for 28 years, had now reached the end of an accountability process, and was in 'Administration'. Our life's work together was now on that downstream barge.

It transpired that the administration process was not as onerous as I had imagined. It had started a month and a half earlier, and was suspended in the Christmas period. We were required to fill in a long form, fully explaining our position, and ultimately our decision to call in the administrators. A 1986 Act of Parliament governs the process, and investigators decide whether or not we have observed the law. We had. We deeply regretted the fact that we left unpaid bills, but most of them were not large. No-one suffered too much as a result of our demise. Most of the capable and loyal members of the company were snapped up by the industries we served with indecent haste. Some had been headhunted over the years and were now free to accept an offer. A few more had jumped ship to other vessels shortly before we sank.

Although we had a rocky period earlier in our history, this time around the problems were more difficult to resolve. Products which had traditionally sold well for us were no longer wanted, and strong competitors were often one step ahead of us. Turnover was spiralling downwards and we could not find the right responses. A further problem had drained both our energy and resolve. My wife and business partner, Sue, had been suffering from cancer for eight years. Three operations in quick succession, as well as a ghastly period of chemotherapy, had failed to stop the evil from spreading. After the first two years, she was pronounced incurable. There were to be no more operations.

With characteristic pragmatism she accepted that her time had run out. Family and friends were told and fingers were crossed. She hoped to still be alive to celebrate a significant birthday later that summer. In the meantime we made the most of life. Long weekends away with friends, as well as some great holidays, were a joy. She seemed quite healthy most of the time. Some amazing new chemotherapy-like drugs were now working well. Specifically they targeted the flow of blood to tumours which had now stopped growing. Our business was well too.

She made it to the birthday party, and then kept going. We continued to live life to the full, and the years rolled on. The cancer years were great for us.

———

Back to the grey day. It was mid-January 2017. The phone call was from the Administrator. The company officially went in to administration on 28th November 2016 but that disaster paled compared to what happened just eleven days after that.

Sue died.

Her body had had enough. After eight years fighting to stay alive, it gave up on her. She was thrilled to have made it out to our eldest son's wedding in Jakarta, Indonesia a few weeks earlier. The wedding photos show Sue smiling, as always, but she was really not well at all. She would not have missed it for the world. Although she made it back to London and was recovering again, the end came with less than two days' notice. She was surrounded by close friends and family, without fear.

———

Slumped against the book cabinet, I glanced away from the window up to a line of framed photos of Sue. She was smiling in some and laughing in others. All of them reminded me of the many great holidays we enjoyed around the world. One in particular took me straight back to perhaps my favourite adventure with her. In the photo, I'm standing in the middle looking charismatic. I wasn't trying to look that way but it's the comment a lot of people have made. My hair is swept back. In fact it's wet because I was sweating so much. Sue is squinting a little towards the camera, and holding her hand above her eyes. The sun was fierce. She never liked the picture as her hair had only just started to grow back after her first period of chemotherapy. Understandably, not a great memory for her. Beside us is our Triumph Rocket III - an early one from 2006. We had owned it from new, adding a customised pillion seat, panniers and intercom to suit our riding needs. We had enjoyed earlier trips on other bikes down to the French riviera, around the Alps and so on. This particular Rocket had given me a self-inflicted scary moment riding the Mountain Course on Mad Sunday at the Isle of Man TT, but later it enjoyed a trip from Land's End to John O'Groats, as well as the Nürburgring, the Alps again, Tuscany, Morocco, Turkey (twice), and now this photo opportunity with Sue. We had flown the Rocket from London to New York, and were heading in a giant zig-zag to finish in Los Angeles, about six weeks later.

We were staying near Salt Lake City, and quite by chance had discovered that the following day was the first day that the Bonneville Salt Flats were declared open for public use that year. So that's where we were when my favourite photograph was taken. You can just ride until the tarmac ends, and hit the salt. It still had a shallow layer of water over much of the surface until late summer. There's a period until late autumn when it's practically dry, and anyone can use it. Speed Week was scheduled for a few weeks after we laid our tracks on it. On the day we were there the Utah Rocket Club were out in the middle of this incredible landscape for their first get together of the year. They were not riding Triumph Rockets, but were sending home made pointed objects, each about two metres tall, into the faultless blue sky. Their rockets were screeching upwards for a mile or so before parachuting safely back to earth. Well, I think that was the idea.

Looking at that photo, which reminded me of all those multi-week adventures with Sue, I just wanted to get back on a bike and keep riding.

REBIRTH

Straightening my back from the slumped position by the book cabinet I began to realise that an opportunity was emerging. It scared me though. Author Ellen Johnson Sirleaf is attributed with writing "The size of your dreams must always exceed your current capacity to achieve them. If your dreams do not scare you, they are not big enough." I am certainly a dreamer but know that most of my dreams were unattainable. Quite possibly many of us have watched a Bond movie and wanted to be 007. If not, we have wanted to be a racing driver, or an Everest climber, or perhaps an overpaid Hollywood movie star. I put my hand up to having wanted to be all of those. Encumbered by responsibilities, work, home, and the endless need for money are amongst the reasons why most people will not have the opportunity to live a dream. Never in my life did I imagine that such an opportunity might present itself to me. Yet it was gradually dawning on me that this opportunity might now exist. Today's phone call meant that I was no longer responsible for running a company. I no longer had an income either, and had also lost at least half my pension plan. My wife of 39 years had died, the mother of our two sons had died, my business partner had died, and my best friend had died. Fuck it! I didn't have much more to lose. I had better go and live my dream before I changed my mind, even if it scared me.

Many of my friends, it transpired, had correctly guessed that I would take some time out, and get on my bike. None though, not even my closest riding buddy, had guessed the scale of my ambition. Finally it was time to announce, with equal amounts of pride and trepidation, that I was setting out to become the first man in the world to ride the world's largest capacity production motorcycle, my 2,300cc. Triumph Rocket X, around the world.

My dream had been fuelled by those who had ventured before me. Thankfully they all chose to communicate their experiences in writing. Excellent books by Ted Simon, Sam Manicom, Jim Rogers and others had all explained to me the importance of opening up my heart and soul, engaging with everyone, and overcoming every difficulty.

I wanted my journey to follow in their footsteps. I did not want it to be just a self-indulgent adventure, though I saw nothing wrong with that if that's all I achieved. I wanted to engage with the world, deliver it some messages, and share some passions. I wanted to give to the world as much of me as I thought it could possibly tolerate. In return, I hoped it would give me something back.

My first message to the world related to Sue's cancer. There's a published list of known causes of her particular cancer, but none of them applied to her. However, it is known that smoking doubles the chance of getting the cancer that she had. She never accepted that smoking was to blame, but that 'double the chance' fact was enough for me to latch on to. So my message was - Please stop smoking, you are all killing yourselves. My second message was much easier for the world to accept - Ride a motorcycle, it can be so much fun. I'm here to prove it.

I also decided to ride with four other passions to share. One was an obvious choice: Triumph Motorcycles. The company is proudly British, and so am I. They design and manufacture a fabulously unique range of exciting products, and I am happy to tell the world how much I love them.

Passion number two: in the past I have been a season ticket holder in the Shed End at Stamford Bridge, London SW6, but I was now just a member of Chelsea Football Club. I know that even when meeting a rival club supporter, there is always a smile to share and a conversation to follow. Football engages more people in the world than any other sport.

Passion number three: I am proud to say that I was at the inaugural meeting of the Ted Simon Foundation in 2011, where I learnt its powerful *raison d'être*. "We believe that individuals of good will, moving among foreign cultures and making themselves vulnerable to the beliefs and customs of strangers, have great importance in promoting world understanding, and even more so when they can distill the essence of their experiences into a form that can be absorbed by many." I was determined to repeat that message to myself as I travelled, and share it with others.

Last, but not least, with a passion for geography, and the way it affects every aspect of history, peoples and cultures, I became a member and supporter of the Royal Geographical Society, then later a Fellow.

I had not lost my home and I had not lost my family and friends, but I had lost just about everything else. However, I was determined to remain positive. I did not allow myself any self-pity. Having had almost six years more than I had expected with Sue I was grateful for the extra time we had together. I did not want sympathy either. I knew that the end was inevitable, and it was not a shock when it happened. Losing the business was a shock though, but largely, or perhaps only, a material one.

Fortunately, I did not lose my Triumph Rocket X either. For me it was the perfect choice for a 'round the world journey, and for many good reasons. Firstly, it was very comfortable. The wide seat, and almost armchair-like riding position suited my frame well. Its colossal weight adds to the comfort too by its ability to absorb potholes and eat tarmac. The weight counts against it when manoeuvring at low speed but I had learnt how to cope with that over the years. I added three new lockable hard plastic panniers, and installed a home-made metal plate in place of the pillion seat. That created just about enough space for everything I wanted to take with me. I also knew the Rocket to be unbreakable. Well, one friend once described the engine as "seriously under-stressed". That comment did wonders for my confidence. Above all, I knew that the Rocket would attract attention wherever I went. All motorcyclists know they are exposed to the world in every possible way. On two wheels, with a motor between your legs or just pedal-power, you are open to everyone and everything around you. There's a two-way opportunity for engagement with other people, whether you are riding along or stopped. The Rocket attracted this attention more than any other bike I had experienced or witnessed. I knew it had the ability to facilitate my engagement with the world.

With decisions about the bike and the passions I wanted to share in place, I now needed to work on myself. I found myself staring out of the window again, at the slightly brighter but still grey sky, looking for answers. I had yet to make some choices about my route, and I had plenty more to do to wrap up what was left of my life in the UK. I was also aware that there were questions I needed to ask about myself. What did I expect from the journey, for example? Forever the dreamer, I had imagined that some new business ideas might present themselves to me as I travelled around the world. In addition, I had thought that working for someone else again might be something to consider too. I also thought that living in another country might very well appeal to me. It was no accident that my ideas about a route would probably take me through France, Italy, Singapore, Australia and the United States at some stage. I had enjoyed previous visits to them all and thought that I should at least now consider living in one of them, if only for a while. More importantly, I had big questions about what was going on in my heart and head. I had developed some prejudices over the years. They needed to go. I'd developed some fears too. They needed to be overcome. I needed to open up my heart and soul to all possibilities and knew that I wouldn't make the most of the journey if I didn't do so.

On a more practical note I needed to make a decision about where to start my journey. I lived in London so I considered the Ace Cafe on the old North Circular Road at Stonebridge Park. It would have suited me well and I am sure they would have been happy to celebrate my departure. But in the end, I decided on the Bike Shed MC in Shoreditch London EC1 since it was more suitable for the majority of my non-biking friends.

I set a date of 1st April 2017. Some thought I was joking.

2. Knock, knock.

"At some point you have to decide to … just go". Wise words I thought, uttered by those who had ventured before me on a motorcycle. I had worked hard to deal with everything in my life that required an original signature on a piece of paper before my departure, but I felt sure that I would think of something else I should have done as soon as I left. I was also aware that there were decisions I still had to make about my route, as well as deal with other inconveniences like insurance, visas and paperwork for the bike. I decided to work the remainder out as I went along. I confess that my optimism was sometimes due to misplaced naivety.

Saturday 1st April 2017 was a crisp, dry spring morning. Two dozen of my closest friends and family had gathered for eggs Benedict, coffee, kisses and tears. Leaving my son, in particular, was difficult. But off I set. An hour later I stopped at my Triumph dealer to meet up with a few more friends, and say goodbye to the team there.

So that was it. Decisions had been made. My past life was now wrapped up in boxes in an attic. Preparations were as complete as I wanted them to be. My trusty steed and I were now on the way, heading west from London. I was happy for a moment, but then suddenly felt alone.

I thought of Sue, and freely confess to crying quite a bit after she died. In fact I was happy when I was crying. Thinking of her whilst immersing myself in photograph collections and memories was an important part of grieving for me. These were private moments. Now I was having one on the bike. Riding whilst crying is not to be recommended. You can't see where you are going! It was to happen a lot from now on, several times a day, triggered by all sorts of memories. I then started to think about my friends and family who had given me so much love and support in the last few months, and realised what a fool I had been. Not only had I removed myself from their lives, and denied them the opportunity to continue to focus their grief for Sue through me, but I had also denied myself the opportunity to continue to receive their love and support. The tears turned to a torrent as I thought "What a fucking idiot you are Mark!". I had to stop.

The afternoon improved. I think that outburst of emotion may have been building up for a while. I found a hotel for the night in Llanelli, Wales, and headed for the port of Fishguard the following morning. Things were to improve from this moment onwards in a way I had not expected. Not at all.

At the port there were a few cars ahead of me to the left, but I was directed to the front of the right hand lane. As I pulled up I noticed a lady, travelling alone, stepping out of her car to stretch her legs for a moment. There was a yellow sign in her side window referring to her status as a grandmother. I asked her if she preferred to be called Gran or Nan. It was Nan. As I was a grandfather-in-waiting I felt I had the right to ask the question. She was easy to talk to in fact. We got on very well and I particularly enjoyed her sense of humour. She made me laugh. Thanks Elaine. For a few moments we talked about all sorts of things. Life, children and grandchildren, work, travel, and our reason for visiting Ireland. We exchanged phone numbers, before being joined by an Irish motorcyclist on a vintage BMW R70/7. His full black leather outfit was vintage too. Mine matched, but was much younger. I spent the crossing talking to him, but could not find Elaine on board. After disembarkation I pulled over for a moment and she drove past, tooting and waving. I did not see her again.

We hooked up with each other that evening on WhatsApp. I had only used the App once before. It had been set up for me to use by a group. This time Elaine had to tell me what to do to make it work. Not only did I discover that it was free to use with wi-fi, but it also felt private. We soon learnt to enjoy each other's secret little messages. We wrote a lot about life and loves, as well as more about our children, her grandchildren, ageing parents, and work again. I soon learnt she was an ardent Arsenal supporter - a 'gooner' - and our mutual love of football helped cement our friendship. As the week in Ireland went by, and our conversations flowed freely, I became discomforted by a feeling of guilt. This was the first time in 40 years that I was at liberty to extend a conversation with another woman. It was unfamiliar territory for me, but I think I was enjoying it.

Considering it is one of the closest countries to my own, I am almost ashamed to admit this was my first visit to Ireland. However I was pleased to discover that people were as friendly as their reputation deserves. It also matched its reputation for lush green landscapes, and rain. I rode clockwise around the island. First stop was Cork, after riding part of the 'copper coast', then Dingle on the west coast. Heading north past Galway towards Sligo I started to see signs for Knock. I knew it was a significant place for Catholics, a destination for pilgrims, but I was not too sure why. I stopped.

Imagine this. A girl thinks she has seen some brightly lit figures near the gable end of a little church. They are almost floating in mid air. She rushes home to fetch her parents. They see the same thing and decide that one of the figures must be 'Our Lady Mary'. Others villagers join the family, and quickly identify the two other figures as Saint Joseph and Saint John. Beside them was a small altar with a lamb standing on it. Don't all lambs love to stand on altars? Above the entire ensemble were some angels with their wings outstretched, forming a halo over the scene. That's what angels do all the time, don't they?

Now I don't wish to be sceptical, I'm not usually so, but I just don't think this is credible. It was in 1879, in a poor and remote area of western Ireland. It was a wet August evening, about 8pm, and the locals might have been on the hooch all day. It doesn't take much of a stretch of the imagination does it? Twenty years earlier another teenage girl had seen a similar apparition in Lourdes, France. It put Lourdes on the map, and tourists, sorry, pilgrims, had been flocking there ever since. The story had plenty of time to reach Ireland.

Some very important people were persuaded to go and investigate. They took testimonies from a wide age range of witnesses, but all of them were Knock villagers. Eventually, the wise important people declared that the testimonies were accurate and credible. It was official. The apparition had indeed taken place, and it was Our Lady Mary. I read some of the testimonies. They didn't mention hooch, but they didn't claim their sobriety either.

Well that was handy. Now their poor remote village started receiving visitors. And so it grew. People flocked there. Even Pope John Paul II and Mother Teresa of Calcutta visited. Now, would you believe it, there's an airport, tarmac, lots of it, a shrine, a basilica, a museum, a hotel, conference rooms, some quite attractive little gardens, and a few statues. There's also plenty of opportunities to have tea and cake in the village, and also buy empty Holy Water bottles.

I don't wish to offend anybody who believes this sort of thing. I truly wish I did. I have observed many times, and fully recognise, that plenty of people around the world gain a huge amount of pleasure from their faith. I have watched Southern Baptists being baptised in the River Jordan, pilgrims crawling on their hands and knees as they come into the Cathedral Square in Santiago de Compostela, and many more. In the 9th.century, Catholic leaders decided that they wanted to bolster support in the north west region of the Iberian peninsula that is now Spain. Conveniently someone found a body buried there and said it was that of the apostle James. They obliged people to go on a pilgrimage to visit it, which they did, and so northern Spain was occupied for catholics, mostly from France. Much cheaper than raising an army. You can go and see his withered blackened digit in the Cathedral if you are so inclined. Irrespective of the finger I think the "pilgrimage" to Santiago is a wonderful thing to do. There are also many non-Christians en route seeking to find something else in their lives, and succeeding.

I am quite content to recognise that religion, anybody's religion, offers hugely important moral guidance to us all. All the little details, like apparitions, just seem to complicate the basics, and separate one religion from another, unnecessarily.

I rode on, entering Northern Ireland for a visit to the Giant's Causeway. Named after a tale in Gaelic mythology it has over 40,000 interlocking basalt columns stretching out to sea - bigger than I had imagined. After enjoying the scenery for another few days I was back in Ireland and headed to Dublin for a pint or two of it's famous stout. I found the legendary Temple Bar. A few glasses of the Black Stuff - it tastes different in Dublin - washed down well with live traditional Irish music. I relished the conversations there with other tourists and a few locals. The experience was not only intoxicating but also challenging for me. I had started to realise that doing things that tourists do, but this time on my own, was not too much fun. I desperately missed not being able to share the experience with someone. All too frequently the thought "I must tell Sue about that as soon as I get home", would flash through my mind before the grave reality of the situation would occur to me.

At the end of my first week I found myself waiting for a ferry to depart once more. This one was heading to Brittany in northern France. Curiously, exactly the same things was about to happen as it did a week before. This time a small blue cocoon of a camper van pulled up beside me. Millie wagged her tale, and Jo stepped out after her. This time it was even easier to start a conversation. There was so much to talk about. The tiny camper van, the tiny bed in view, her dog, the romany - esque curtains, the cosily assembled interior, and Jo herself, dressed to my mind a little like a bohemian hippy. I don't remember which came first but I rattled through all of the obvious questions, as well as talking a little about myself, just in time to board the ferry. We shared a bottle of wine on board, and I left her to settle Millie down for the night in her cage on the 'poop' deck. The following morning we met for breakfast together in Roscoff, followed by a glorious walk along the beach. The conversation moved easily from one subject to another. She was in Brittany for some wwoofing. A new word in my dictionary. Wwoofers visit organic farms to live and work there for a week or so. She also loved her impromptu music sessions in pubs, or french bars. We agreed to meet up again in Locronan, a well preserved late middle age village. Jo checked in to the camper van parking area, and I checked in to a simple hotel. We enjoyed a stroll around the village, a drink in a bar, a walk down a lane and around some fields for Millie's benefit, and eventually a meal in my hotel. Before returning to her camper van in the dark, she checked that she had her keys to hand. They weren't there. They were on a lanyard which was always wrapped around the buckle of her handbag's shoulder strap, before the key ring bundle itself was placed inside her bag. The method seemed faultless, but nevertheless there was nothing there. She looked quite terrified, but explained that there was another set inside her camper, and felt confident enough that the bent coat hanger trick might work to open the door, if all else failed. We set off with our phones on the torch setting, retracing our steps around the village and fields, twice. Enquiries at a couple of bars proved fruitless too. So, being the perfect English gentleman that I am, I suggested we continued the search in the morning, but in the meantime I offered to share my hotel bedroom with her, and Millie of course. There was a caveat to my offer: the room was small and only had one bed.

Do I have to tell you the English gentleman behaved impeccably?

In the morning we returned to her van to break into it. With the help of some fellow campers, we succeeded. Visibly relieved, she accepted my invitation to enjoy a coffee and croissant together before parting. We turned to walk back across the car park. I glanced upward for a second and shrieked. There were her original keys, with lanyard, hanging from the wing mirror of a larger van. Somebody must have found them and hung them up at eye level. Very considerate; we should have looked higher, but were only looking for them on the ground in the dark with a torch.

REBIRTH

The coffee and croissants were particularly good, but it was time to say goodbye. I din't see Jo again. Instead I headed south, then across France, and eventually to Barcelona. It was Easter weekend.

Two things particularly excited me about being there. One, I love cities. The bigger the better. They are full of people, and all of them fascinate me. Over Easter I could be certain that the town was going to be full, and I could also observe the religious street parades over the weekend. I would surely learn something. Secondly, I had managed to get a ticket to see FC Barcelona play at the Camp Nou. My religion. Apart from the improving spring weather in Europe, my second reason for leaving the UK at this time was to give me an opportunity to visit as many of the great football stadia as I could before the season ended in late May. The thought of the enormous Camp Nou, the largest stadium in Europe, thrilled me. Lionel Messi scored twice, as Barcelona beat Real Sociedad 3:2. It was not until late in the second half though that I realised the stadium design did not include a roof. It started to rain, but I went home with a smile anyway.

A warm sunny day followed and helped me to enjoy Gaudi's extraordinary buildings and the Sagrada family Basilica, as well as a moment to reflect on Christopher Columbus at the bottom of the La Ramblas, the principal street for tourists to amble in Barcelona.

There is a rather splendid statue to him there, standing sixty metres on top of a column. Proudly erected there by the people of Barcelona in 1888 he stands as tall as many a man on a column, pointing with his arm outstretched to sea. Nursery rhymes, history books, and many of my American friends have had me believe most of my adult life that he "discovered" America. In fact, Columbus did not discover, or even visit, the landmass we now call North America.
Whereas he was an accomplished sailor and navigator, and most certainly crossed the Atlantic from Europe, four times in fact, he only found some Caribbean islands, and turned south. He eventually landed in Venezuela. His legacy though is significant

in that there has been a continuous flow of trans-Atlantic voyages since him. He enabled the patriation of America by Europeans.

Although born in Genoa, Italy, Columbus was funded by the Spanish Monarchy, hence his journeys are commemorated in Spain. He was sent to find a shorter route to the spice islands of the 'East Indies'. He didn't, but that's another story.

History records that the viking explorer Leif Erikson crossed the Atlantic successfully in the 11th. Century, landing in Newfoundland, Canada. Centuries before that Chinese and Japanese explorers landed on the west coast of North America.

To find out why Columbus has been popularised as the "discoverer" of America we have to look no further back than 1776, in my view, when John Adams, Thomas Jefferson, and others published the Declaration of Independence (from the British). At the time their contemporaries thought it would be useful to rally popular support behind a 'hero'. They could not choose John Cabot, even though he definitely crossed from Britain to land on the North American continent in 1497. He too was Italian, from Venice, (Giovanni Caboto), but was funded and supported by Henry VII, the English King. The hero had to be non-English, so Columbus was chosen. A good choice of course as USA won and Britain lost.

On Easter Sunday I strolled around the centre of the city again, observing some of the parades and large wooden effigies of Christ on the cross. Some of the crosses were covered in red roses. After lunch I felt a little jaded and sat down for a rest on a low wall in a narrow side street. The sun found a gap between the buildings, and warmed me in my little spot. I felt somewhat detached form everyone else. After a while I realised I was sat by the entrance to a church - Santa Maria. I ventured through the door and found myself walking straight up the aisle. What happened next took me completely by surprise. Utterly oblivious to anyone else except myself, I continued up the aisle and sat in the first pew on the right. I glanced up at the stained glass windows above the alter, now sharing the same little shaft of light that I had been enjoying outside. At this moment, I burst into tears. I do literally mean burst. I was out of control. I was in a trance. My eyes were shut but still the shower flowed. I could have been there for five minutes or even thirty; I honestly don't know.

Sue and I had a stained glass window moment together a few years earlier. We were visiting the Abbey at St. Foy in Conques, central France. A monk escorted us on an early evening tour, pointing out the contemporary glasswork for which it had also become famous. He left us to walk around again on our own whilst he started to play traditional church music on the organ. Sue was ahead of me and had sat down in a pew. As I descended a staircase to join her, the monk changed his repertoire. He started to play "House of the Rising Sun" by The Animals. Sue and I had been playing it quite a lot in the car on this particular trip. It reminded her of her youth, and had become a favourite once more during her cancer years. I sat down beside her, and, glancing over, realised she was crying.

During her funeral service I had also recollected the Conque moment when glancing up at the stained glass windows in St. Luke's, Chelsea. I managed to retain some composure then, but this time the emotion gushed out. When I returned to being at least semiconscious, I realised that Santa Maria in Barcelona was huge, and filled with dozens of tourists. No one came over to try and console me, not even the clergy. I was probably unconsolable anyway. The tissue in my pocket was no good to me either. My T-shirt was soaking.

I stepped outside and after another short walk I found a park. I lay down on a grass bank and fell asleep with my camera bag under my head, exhausted. Children woke me later. They were playing inside the bushy hedge beside me. I heard music too. In fact lots of it. There were small groups with banjos, guitars, and accordions. Some had wi-fi speakers playing music from their phones. Everybody was happy. Enterprising vendors were urgently moving amongst us selling chilled drinks including beer. I walked amongst them too, still slightly disconnected from the real world, but happier also. A crowd of African musicians were playing drums, extremely energetically. Others had strapped slackline webs between trees, just a metre off the ground, and were bouncing on them as if they were trampolining. My extraordinary couple of hours left me leaving Cuitadella Park with a spring in my step too.

It wasn't until a few days later that I was able to reflect on the tearful outburst. Thoughts of Sue still filled my heart as I continued to ride along, but I was now able to control my tears. There were watery eye moments, but not longer floods. Easter Sunday had been pivotal in my grieving process, but I didn't think it was a religious moment.

--- --- ---

I rode south, following the Spanish coast, trying to make sense of my life. At times, thoughts moved around freely inside my helmet. It's a great space for me. Almost anything could trigger a series of random musings. It might be a town name, a crop in a field, something for lunch, a smell, or even someone twiddling with their hair as Sue did. They would each take me down memory lane with her or perhaps lead me to speculate about my life in the future. They would often take me away from thinking about the road in front of me, but somehow I still seemed to be making progress safely enough. I reached the Costa del Sol and stayed with friends for a few days. Conversations flowed generously from both sides, but I was at last able to stop and take a breath with them. I had not done that since the previous summer, or perhaps it was almost nine years ago when Sue was well.

A few days later I was stretched out again on a beach in Portugal, just relaxing. It was there that I realised to my amusement that a single man on a beach on his own, attracts other single men on a beach on their own. Not for me. I sought couples to talk to, and more women of course. This hadn't happened on a beach, but was easy enough at times in restaurants. In Cordoba, Spain, heading north again, it happened on consecutive nights in the same restaurant. The single lady was also staying in my hotel around the corner. We got on well, exchanging life stories for a few hours, just as I had done earlier at the ferry ports to and from Ireland. These encounters were definitely adding an extra dimension to my journey. I was tempted to wonder whether or not chasing women around the world might be an exciting way to continue.

Cordoba had been developed by the Romans as it had all the geographical elements they liked in a town. It still displays much evidence from the period, but it is "La Mezquita" which I found most intoxicating. An immense mosque built by successive Moorish leaders features some glorious architecture including columned halls. A catholic church was later built inside it, and the entirety is now enveloped in the narrow streets of the Jewish quarter. A matador museum was a ghoulish experience, but added to the fascination of the city. I left looking forward to further visits to the Roman and Moorish cities of Andalusia one day.

Next stop was Madrid to watch Christiano Ronaldo and Real Madrid play Valencia at the Bernabeu stadium. The architecture is not Moorish, nor Roman, but felt like a coliseum to me. When the visitors equalised late in the second half Ronaldo raised his game and it was all over a few minutes later. 2:1. His stance was gladiatorial. Central Spain was still cool and wet as I continued north and over the Pyrenees. The roads were clear but with plenty of snow on both sides.

A dilemma had started to build up for me as I thought about my route around the north of the Mediterranean towards Italy. I was likely to end up near Cassis, a little beyond Marseille. Cassis was a very special place for Sue and I. We had been going there for many years, sometimes for weekends and at other times for longer. It had become our favourite bolt-hole. We would shoot down there on a bike when life, or perhaps the pressure of business, had built up. We flew once, and took the train on another occasion. The hotels were all adequate, but the small port teemed with great little fish restaurants. The odd wet day allowed us to walk along the paths of the Calanques or perhaps a bit further, but we spent most of our days on one of several secluded rocky beaches. I took the plunge and booked to stay there. It fact this was to be my first Airbnb booking. I recognised the location from the description, but was quite taken aback when I arrived to discover it was immediately next door to a room I had stayed in once before. The room was small and simple but had everything I needed, including it's direct view of the quayside, port, and castle beyond.

I spent the first day walking around town for a while. A few of the bars seemed to have changed hands but otherwise everything was familiar. A sandwich and drink was all I needed to take to my beach for a few hours in the afternoon. The warmth of summer was still a few weeks away, but I lay there comfortably enough with a book. The space beside me was empty; I didn't like that. In the evening I chose to eat at my all-time favourite *soupe de poisson* restaurant. They offer plenty of great sounding appetisers, but from the first visit onwards I never ordered anything else. Fresh fish of the day and creme caramel followed, all washed down with a crisp local white. The proprietor recognised me as my surname always amused him. His wife's dog was older than I remember.

The following day was a repeat of the first. I felt quite comfortable in Cassis, as always, even without my little friend beside me. Every corner of the town held a memory of our holidays together but, although I was not sure why, I seemed to be quite comfortable there once more. Perhaps it was the familiarity that helped. However, on this particular evening I chose a new restaurant. This one had not been open long when we were last there, but had been enjoying a growing reputation. I made a reservation for one, and arrived early enough to be offered a table with my back to the wall. I always liked to be able to 'people watch' if possible. The restaurant was small and cosy; Muriel and Lionel made me feel very welcome. As usual, the place setting in front of me was cleared away. I gave my order, including a good bottle of wine, and started to enjoy the foie gras with toasted brioche. As I did so, three other guests arrived and sat at a round table for four in front me. As with my table, the redundant place setting was cleared away, leaving me with a clear view. My people watching opportunities this evening were complete. To my left, there was a table of four, with two young ladies and an older couple. The gentleman, my age, was the host. They were celebrating a birthday. To my right were two tables of two with couples deeply engrossed in each other's company. The far side of the restaurant had a similar layout and clientele. However, with my head down, my eyes flipped up and back again in quick succession as I tried to figure out the table in front of me. There was a gentleman on the right, a lady with light brown hair in the middle, and a blonde haired lady to the left. They were all about the same age, but I could not figure out the relationships. They clearly knew each other well, and seemed to have enjoyed or drink or two somewhere else before reaching the restaurant. My main course was served. Fish again, but fresh and delicious. The wine was going down well. My eyes flipped up again at the table opposite, but this time I was spotted. The lady in the middle was smiling at me. It was a huge smile accompanied by bright nut brown eyes. Her head was tilted slightly. I turned away, but back again in a minute, only to be caught again. The blonde haired lady was smiling too, and the brown haired lady now had her thumb and forefinger to her lips and was encouraging me to smile. I knew I looked miserable when I was eating alone, and was grateful for the fact she was trying to improve my evening. But I was aware that they were all speaking french at considerable speed, and an invitation for me to join them a moment later terrified me. I spoke *franglais* at best, despite numerous visits to the country over the years. I was taught french at school but now could only speak just enough to get by as a tourist. I ordered another bottle of my wine with desert, and after the third invitation, and ever widening smiles, I picked up my bottle and took two paces across the restaurant to join them. *"Bonsoir"*, I announced, *"Je m'appelle Mark, et je suis anglais"*. They recoiled, having had no idea that was the case. I sat down nervously. Their smiles widened again. The lady in the middle, the one with the light brown hair, replied *"Je m'appelle Dalila"*. I asked her to repeat it as I was not sure I had heard her correctly. I had never met anyone called Dalila in my life. She explained that it was french for Delilah. She then introduced me to the blonde haired lady next to her. Her name was Dalila too. "You've got to be kidding me" was written all over my face, and visible in any language. Two Dalila's had just arrived in my life at the same time.

I half expected the gentleman to be called Dalila too, but was relieved to learn it was Jean-Philipe. His smile was polite, but I wondered if I had spoilt his evening by interfering with the still unfathomable relationship with the two ladies. I later learned that they were all just friends. In fact six of them had been on holiday together in a rented house nearby, with just the three of them left for their final night.

All things considered we managed to converse quite effectively, covering the basics about each other using simple words and sentences. The wine and smiles helped. So too did the glint in the eyes of both the ladies. They whispered to each other whilst looking at me, probably returning a similar glint by now. The two Dalilas, the blonde now being referred to as Dali, then broke into song. Bob Dylan's classic, "I want you". We all laughed, nervously. The restaurant was now empty, so we paid and stepped out into the narrow alley. Strolling down to the port they took me in their arms and invited me to join them for more drinks back at their house. With the courage given to me by too much wine, I din't hesitate to accept, but remembered that the last time I did something like this was when I was about 20.

Jean-Philipe drove us the few miles along the coast, and the evening continued with yet more drinks. My memory fades with alcohol but I think that I eventually crashed out on a sofa. I was certainly there in the morning, feeling rough. The ladies appeared with coffee, thankfully several cups.

Although it was Dali who latched on to me the night before, it was Dalila and I who couldn't stop talking to each other in the morning. The conversation was warm, easy and soft. Their lounge was spacious with plenty of early morning sunlight pouring in through two huge bay windows. They were wide open as Dalila and I perched on the edge of a low sill. She explained to me that Paul Cezanne, the late 19th. century artist, as well as his contemporaries, used to stroll along the footpath below our window. It meandered through pine trees above the sandy beach and bay beyond, known as La Madrague. I stared silently into her eyes as she spoke. Something exploded inside me.

We exchanged WhatsApp details as we made our way back to Cassis, and took one more coffee in a cafe. Then she was gone. She went back to Lyon where she lives. As I floated back along the quay to my apartment, still in something of an alcoholic stupor, I chanced upon the couple who had been on the table of four to my left in the restaurant the night before. They roared with laughter and gave each other a nudge with their elbows, signaling that I must have had a good evening with the girls. I had.

Back in my little room, the WhatsApp conversations with Dalila started straight away, this time with the assistance of Google Translate. In the afternoon I strolled around town rather than going to the beach again, and took an early night after a simple bite to eat. By the following morning the hangover had gone, but the conversations with her were in full swing.

I tried hard but failed to get a ticket to watch Juventus play at home in Turin, but succeeded in getting one to watch AC Milan at the San Siro stadium. Looking at a map, I realised that I had probably enough time to divert to Lyon en route to Milan. After plucking up the courage I invited myself to visit her, and was thrilled to receive a positive reply. In fact, she did not hesitate. I shot straight up the motorway, and was greeted by that fabulous smile, and slight tilt of the head.

Her home is in the dead centre of Lyon so it was easy to enjoy a stroll around some of the sights together in the afternoon. An early evening 'apero' went down well, and a glorious meal at her favourite restaurant topped off the day beautifully. I stayed the night. In the morning we enjoyed breakfast together in the main square and I left for Milan saying: "Thank you for a lovely time, but you do know I have to continue my journey around the world". After all, I was only just 5 weeks into it.

.

3. *Vai, Vivi e Ritorno.*

The ride over the Alps was distinctly cold and wet. My modest hotel booking in Milan did little to warm me, but an evening in a restaurant opposite proved joyful. I met a young honeymooning couple from Texas. They effervesced with their description of their wedding day. I almost spoilt their evening telling them why I was travelling around the world on my own. In fact, they seemed quite taken by my story and congratulated me for my positivity. This was the first of many similar reactions to my journey. I bumped into them the following night at the San Siro, and we have remained friends.

The game was not the best. AC Milan were beaten 4:1 by Roma, and the atmosphere reflected the lack-lustre performance on the pitch. The stadium is a glorious design, quite unique, but inside the experience was disappointing. Locals smoked freely in front of and beside me, whilst a couple of policemen smoked equally freely right by the no smoking sign.

I rode down Italy, passing places that were already familiar to me, but stopped again for a few days on the Amalfi coast at Maiori. I learnt that the Romans used to be tourists here too, but wondered if any of them had journeyed on their own. Surely this romantic coastline was best enjoyed even then with a loved one, or family and friends. I felt alone, and decided this would be the last time that I planned to take a break in a coastal resort again.

I continued south, hopping over to Sicily, then to Malta, where I stayed with friends for a few days. They were great hosts, introducing me to their friends, showing me the sights, and filling me with sumptuous food and wine.

By now though, the conversations with Dalila had stepped up a level. I had learnt that she liked Italy, and wondered if spending some more time with me there would appeal to her, somewhere on my journey back up the country. She chose Rome and accepted my choice of room in the central historic district for a few days. We had a glorious time together, enjoying each other's company whilst feasting on the architecture, monuments, history and culture of ancient Rome. It's a very romantic city! More importantly, we realised that we were extremely compatible. On almost every topic we held the same opinion. Although we had both led quite different lives, we had arrived at the same moment with the same outlook. Conversation after conversation concluded in accord. We remarked on the conclusion every time, and were delighted by it. Something was stirring inside, for both of us.

We both adored our visit to the Colosseum, truly one of the great wonders of the world. The scale of the structure is as remarkable as the way it was used. Notorious for its gladiatorial encounters, it also hosted other sporting events, as well as parades of animals and objects collected from around the Roman Empire. I concluded that the atmosphere inside might have been comparable to that of a modern stadium, which I freely admit to enjoying so much.

Parting at Rome's airport proved surprisingly difficult for me. It ended, as it did in Lyon, with me saying "Thank you, that was great, but you know I am still going to continue my journey around the world". I stood in a trance as she went through passport control, unable to move my jellied legs for a few minutes, wishing I had paid more when given the opportunity to toss a coin and make three wishes at the Trevi Fountain. I recalled the first wish. *'Vai, vivi e ritorno'*. Go, live and return. The second wish was to allow you to have a new romance. I didn't get to three.

I packed my bike and left Rome for Siena, enjoying a night overlooking the famous Piazza del Campo, and another great Italian meal. On to Venice and another fabulous conversation with an American couple in a restaurant. Not honeymooners this time, but celebrating a significant wedding anniversary instead. They were from Ohio, well travelled too, and knew the north of

Italy well. Via social media they remained avid and faithful supporters of my journey.

Over the years I have enjoyed relaxing on nudist beaches from time to time. Some were officially designated for the purpose, but most were not. I have also been on campsites many times. However, I have never previously combined the two.

Croatia has a long history of supporting naturism, so I booked 4 nights on one of the most established, and certainly one of the largest campsites. It had 1500 plots and the website successfully lured me with tasteful photos of healthy looking young people. Imagine my disappointment after I checked in to discover that I was the youngest one there! Almost all of the other naturists were retired Germans, with a few from Austria, Holland and Portugal. I was not only the sole British visitor, but the only solo camper too.
As soon as I pulled up the Rocket they started fussing over me with the usual questions. How big is that engine? How many cylinders? Where have I been travelling? Where am I going? Am I alone? Only this time I was answering the questions in the nude.
It did not take long, an hour maybe, before I realised that they were showering me with admiration and love. Can they help me set up the tent? Would I like a cup of tea? Would I like to join them later for a beer? Their age, (their obesity), and our nudity, all quickly became irrelevant. Or perhaps it was relevant. I was not sure.
When you are all naked, there is nowhere to hide. We are all reduced to the lowest common denominator. That encourages engagement with each other in a way I had never previously been aware. It was a wonderful feeling.
I joined a small group of friends for drinks. They knew each other well and had been coming to the same place for decades. I was the genuinely welcome stranger in their midst. They spoke almost no English, and I spoke even less German. Nevertheless we managed to discuss a terrific range of topics moving from the

pleasures of eating fresh grilled fish, to the mood swings of Jose Mourinho. If you focus on their eyes, the other 'bits' disappear. In a further conversation I was impressed to learn that a few of them still came there even when the Balkan war was on. They listened to low flying bombers roar overhead every night from bases in Italy.

At regular intervals I found myself re-thinking the purpose of my journey. Searching for something of a new life for myself, somehow, didn't seem to be as important to me as delivering the messages I had for the world. Wherever the Rocket and I stopped, a conversation would follow on almost every occasion. With varying degrees of success I tried to introduce those messages whenever possible. The stickers on the back of the top-box helped. Chelsea Football Club came up quite a lot. Fellow supporters were delighted to see the club logo, and often spotted it at quite a distance. Rival supporters would still grin. Chelsea had just been crowned Premier League Champions, but had lost the FA Cup final to Arsenal. Elaine was happy. It was also easy to talk about Triumph Motorcycles. After all, they had built this colossal beast which was going to carry me faithfully around the world. Very few people wanted to talk to me about the Please Stop Smoking sticker on the bike, though. Immediately, smokers would tell me why they had to continue their habit. They closed their mind to my message as soon as I started to explain why it was there. Of course they offered sympathy when I said "Sue smoked. Sue got cancer. Sue died". I became quite comfortable with using that phrase. It was blunt, but succinct. Everybody knows people who had died from smoking related diseases, but only a few people admitted that to me. Smokers themselves would tell me it was not easy to give up, and even resented my attempt to interfere with their lives. It was their choice, they told me. At least no-one tried to tell me that smoking was good for them. Eventually I posted my feelings on the subject on social media in a series of three messages. It didn't help. Nobody told me they would try again to give up, and the Cancer Research donation page I set up in Sue's name received little support. I was happy to talk about the Royal Geographical Society and the Ted Simon Foundation but found very few people who were familiar with either. They listened politely for a moment but I doubt if my words were of much help to anybody.

Something else struck me about Croatia which came as quite a surprise. Whilst riding along the motorway which runs roughly parallel to the coast, but inland along the ridge of a mountain range, I noticed a succession of short tunnels over the road, all with a particular sign beside them. I slowed to read one of them, then had to stop at the next to make sure I had read it correctly. Yes I had. These were not tunnels at all, but bridges, built specifically to allow bears and wolves to pass over them. I looked more carefully at the next couple and realised that the tunnels had more than enough earth over the top of them to support trees and bushes, which in turn blended well with the wider landscape. Bravo Croatia. Not only had you supported your wildlife, but learnt that they will thrive on their own without interfering with yours.

Bosnia had a town that I particularly wanted to see. Mostar. During the awful Balkan war it became the focus of attention because its bridge, set high above a gorge, ran through the middle of the town. Waring factions decided this would be a good place to focus their divisive efforts. After fierce fighting and thousands of deaths the bridge was blown up. The Stari Most, or Old Bridge, plunged spectacularly into the river below on the evening of 9th. November 1993. Quite by chance, I had booked myself into a small guest house nearby, whose owner had been the one to capture the famous event on video. His young nephew described to me how terrified his ancestors were during this period of intense fighting. Many fled the town, but they stayed as long as they could, barricaded in by sand bags. The late 16th. century Ottoman masterpiece had been reconstructed and was now the focus of attention for tourists. The young nephew also told me that jumping off the bridge was a right of passage for the adolescent males of Mostar. It was a dangerous plunge of twenty-five metres, into icy shallow waters. Aged fifteen he managed it and survived, but admitted he had no intention of going anywhere near the outside edge again.

My passage through Montenegro was uneventful, except for it's border controls. It was not a member of the EU, and demanded I paid for a kind of *'carte gris'* road insurance. Europe's opulence all but disappeared on entering Albania. Buildings were scruffy, fields were smaller, and roads were unkept. Eventually, my first substantial period on an unpaved road slowed me down and forced me to make a u-turn to find somewhere to stay earlier than I had expected that day. It also gave me a delightful surprise. I rode up slowly behind a heard of six cows with an elderly herds-woman in charge. She shouted something at her six ladies and tapped her stick to the ground. Three of them dutifully went to the left side of the road, and three went to the right. In unison, the cows glanced over their shoulders as I carefully went past them. I nodded my thanks to the old lady and she nonchalantly shouted one more word back at the cows. In my mirror I watched with amazement again as they returned to their formation in the middle of the road. Udderly remarkable.

Greece was easy riding once more and allowed me to quickly get to Nafplio on the Peloponnese peninsula. I met with friends and thoroughly enjoyed their company for a couple of days, taking in a visit to the ancient city of Epidaurus whilst there. They suggested an onward route for me via Lesbos, a Greek island close to Turkey. I accepted, and took an overnight ferry from Athens. Although I had a quick look around the island on the internet, I arrived with no accommodation booked, and headed off to follow the coast for a while. A small town, with a couple of small hotels to chose from, was all I needed. My choice turned out to be delightful, totally Greek, and with great hospitality from the owners. However, the summer season was not yet evident, but austerity following Greece's financial crisis most definitely was. There was little prospect of a successful summer season to follow. It was all a bit too quiet for me so I headed to a larger town. More people, fish restaurants along the promenade, and a beach with other tourists, was much more interesting for me. I renegaded on a promise I had made to myself in Portugal, and spent a day on the beach with a book. A young lady, on her own, with an impossibly flat stomach, said hello. She spoke good English. We sipped a couple of beers together whilst the sun went down, and for a few more hours enjoyed each other's company over a meal. I saw her the following day on the back of a young man's motorbike and shouted "But my bike's bigger than his!". We both laughed.

On another night, in a restaurant, I happened to notice that all the other tables were occupied by female couples. I amused myself by recalling the schoolboy joke. "Where do lesbians go on their holiday?" "Lesbos". I chatted to the restaurant owner for a while, and asked her if indeed it was true. She raised her eyebrows in acknowledgement. I later learnt that it stemmed from an ancient greek poet called Sappho who lived on the island. Around 2500 years ago she wrote about her love for a woman. In fact much of her work has been lost, but fragments confirm this was the case. Quite enough for lesbians to latch on to and go there for their holidays.

It was only a short ferry ride over to the Turkish port of Ayvalik. I knew from previous trips that I would need to buy another *'carte gris'* at the border, but learnt when I got there that was no longer possible. Apparently there were not enough foreigners arriving in their own vehicle to support the need for an insurance office. After several fruitless hours trying to negotiate a solution, I had to take the late afternoon ferry back to Lesbos. A day later I took another ferry to the northern Greek mainland port of Kaval, for my ride east to one of Turkey's major entry points for road traffic. They let me in. I entered the country with belching trucks, crazy road habits and at long last a feeling that my adventure was truly beginning.

4. Bosphorus and bullets.

Heading for an exit from Europe I decided to firm up my planned route. Very broadly I intended to head in a south-easterly direction until I reached New Zealand. My route would take me through Turkey, Iran, Dubai, India, Nepal, Myanmar, Thailand, Cambodia, Malaysia, Singapore, Indonesia and Australia. The first obstacle would be Iran. UK, as well as US and Canadian citizens needed both a visa and an official guide to accompany them at all times. I had managed to find an organisation in the UK who offered to arrange the guiding service. It started with asking the Tehran authorities for permission to apply for a visa. Once the permission was given, the visa process itself was little more than an administrative one, but required me to present the application and my passport at an Iran Consulate. I left London without it and subsequently chose the Consulate in Istanbul. Entering Turkey, the permission to apply step had still not been given. It was made clear to me that there was nothing I could do to control the timing of that process. This was an unfamiliar feeling for me. As a businessman I was more used to at least having some control of everything I wanted to do.

I arrived on the outskirts of the vast metropolis that is Istanbul, and progressed with ever diminishing speed to the very centre. My apartment reservation was in the tourist district of Sultanahmet which I managed to find in the midst of some vertiginous cobbled streets, without dropping the Rocket on any of its tight corners. I met my host and immediately received disappointing news. The football season had finished that very day and I would not be able to visit either Fenerbahce, Besiktas or Galatasaray. That was the end of my football aspirations for a while.

However, there was sensational news to follow. Dalila confirmed she was able to come out and join me in a couple of days. Our WhatsApp conversations had continued with ever increasing enthusiasm. We had not only been in contact every day, but now several times a day. I was over the moon.

In recent weeks I had been drip-feeding news of her entry into my life to some close friends. They were all thrilled for me, but offered caution. In fact I realised already how vulnerable my heart might be at this moment in my life, acknowledging that strong emotions were still gushing through my system alarmingly. I had still not found the courage to mention anything about Dalila to my close family, who made it clear in every communication how much they were still grieving. I was still the focus of their grief.

Further good news followed. I could now go to the Iran Consulate with my permission to apply for a visa. They had a well guarded building near the Topkapi Palace, close to my the apartment. I approached the brass plaque on the wall with a certain amount of trepidation, hoping that I wouldn't slip up if any searching questions were asked. In fact the whole process was efficient, polite and cordial, and even included a few smiles. I was not yet there but felt welcome already.

———

During the first couple of days in Istanbul I wandered around on my own, counting down the hours until Dalila's arrival. Celebrating another one of life's 'significant birthdays' was not high on my list but nevertheless I felt quite lonely when it happened on 12th. June. I had expected to be alone so couldn't complain to anyone. Family and friends sent me messages, and a couple even managed to phone me.

My wanderings gave me enough of an insight into the city to be able to efficiently hit the streets on the tourist trail the following day. I met Dalila at the airport, relieved to see me after a delayed flight. We lapsed into easy conversation straight away and enjoyed a spectacular roof top view from my chosen restaurant that first evening. We were both excited by each other's company, as well as intoxicated by the atmosphere around us. Ramadan was being observed during this period, and entertained us with a sudden rush of activity and feasting as fast broke each evening.

We were staying directly opposite a mosque, whose outer wall was almost touchable from our apartment window. In total I stayed there for two weeks and became quite accustomed to the call to prayer up to five times a day. However, it was the one which announced the end of the fast each day which attracted the biggest rush of people, almost entirely male. Many of the city's women and children had already left their homes to occupy a picnic spot to take their Iftar, the meal at the end of the day's fast, preferably on the grass in a park or a bench in the areas surrounding public buildings, which were almost exclusively mosques. As a symbol of abundance, dates are often eaten before a meal; fresh, dried, or chocolate covered. Yummy.

Built in the sixth century AD on the European side of the Bosphorus river, the Hagia Sofia features a huge dome visible not just from the Asia side, but by all river traffic. It was originally built as a Greek Orthodox Cathedral before being adopted as a mosque. Now a museum, it houses some interesting artwork, but its scale, grandeur and history seem to delight visitors more than anything. My personal preference is for the Sultan Ahmed Mosque next door, also known as the Blue Mosque, built 1000 years later. It covers a greater area with five large central domes, eight smaller ones, and six minarets. Many of the interior walls and columns are covered in beautiful blue hand painted tiles, which reflect their colour and cast a calm light over the red carpet below. I was highly amused by a sign near to where men carry out their ablutions: 'The place of ablution for ladies is at the backside'.

The famous Grand Bazaar felt chaotic at the outset, with over 4,000 shops and at least 250,000 visitors every day, but is in fact highly organised. Life inside the world's largest shopping mall has a well practised and orderly routine, best observed by taking a step back and just watching it all happen. Like so many bazaars around the world it started as a meeting place for traders, offering a huge range of goods including, gold, textiles, food and spices. It was simple enough for Ottoman traders to thrive here, with full control of all east west activities. The quality of the displays allowed the merchandisers to elevate their art form to the highest levels I have ever seen.

We visited the Galata Tower which gave us yet another magnificent view of the city, as well as the Topkapi Palace. A boat trip up the Bosphorus river gave us another fabulous experience, observing frenetic activity by every kind of vessel from huge sea containers to tiny pleasure craft. It was only twenty miles long but the whole of its length had turned a bizarre shade of turquoise when we were there. It was later explained that there had been a growth explosion of a particular plankton full of white calcium carbonate, now feeding down from the Black Sea. The boat stops to allow for a walk to a view point, and was followed by an excellent fish lunch in the hill top restaurant. We were interrupted, and surprised to hear a rustle in the bushes beside us, followed by a man with a camera in his hand emerging from it, brushing himself down, and mounting a rustic fence to climb into our restaurant. He stopped for a moment to explain that he likes to find different view points, and often chances his luck to do so. He disappeared down the hill as quickly as he had arrived. By chance I met him again in a restaurant in the centre of the city a few days later. He had not climbed in this time. We chatted for an hour or so, and exchanged life histories. I found him very interesting and enjoyed hearing about some of his other exploits around the world.

Derek, an Australian from near Melbourne, told me about his succinct views on being a "Good Traveler". For many years he had travelled to some of the most interesting, extraordinary and remote places on the planet, making himself vulnerable to its idiosyncrasies and cultures. He insists on taking alternate paths to most tourists. In fact he says he is not a tourist but a traveller. He had developed a '4 Goods' philosophy.

Good Planning: he suggests that you should have a good idea of where you are going, why you are going there, and what you expect or hope to experience. Without planning you will waste time, and possibly miss out on the true value of the location. It sounds obvious really but I am sure we are all liable to not do this well enough on some occasions. I certainly am.

Good Luck: he acknowledges that sometimes things happen beyond our control. This might range from the taxi driver who takes you the longer route to charge you more, to the bus driver who falls asleep at the wheel and crashes. Perhaps a military coup might start whilst you are there, or an earthquake, or a cancelled flight. These things are beyond a traveller's control and only by being lucky can you avoid them. Good luck.

Good People: This category he divides into two. Firstly, those good people who serve you well. The hotelier, the restaurateur, the tour guide and so on who deliver you excellent service, above and beyond just doing their job. Secondly, the good people who have absolutely nothing to gain from helping you. They just want to help. They give you directions and advice, offer you a cup of tea, or even a meal and a bed for the night. These are the people who make adventure travel such a joy. I sing their praises, and wholeheartedly agree with my fellow traveller.

Good Intentions: he says we should all start off with respect for those we meet, to show an interest in them and their culture, as well as the environment they live in.

He invited me to visit him at his home near Melbourne, Australia if I made it that far. I accepted.

Dalila and I rounded off our week and a half in Istanbul with a little shopping, and continued with great conversations, one after the other. The warm, easy relationship was spoilt by yet another difficult departure at the airport. I said goodbye, as before, by saying "Thank you, that was great, but you know I still have to continue my journey around the world". I was heading to Iran next.

I crossed the Bosphorus, visiting the Triumph dealer on the other side for a small seal to be replaced, and continued east, deeper into Asia. Next stop was Goreme in the centre of a region called Cappadocia. The landscape was full of cone shaped rock formations known as fairy chimneys. Thousands of them defined

the character of the centre of the town, and were also scattered throughout several valleys. They had been carved for a rich variety of reasons, collecting guano being one of them. Not my favourite. Others had rooms, houses and even castles cut into them. Some date back over 1000 years, and run deep underground to create secure floors below the surface, whilst others have the advantage of a high view above ground level.
Something extraordinary happens there every morning throughout the year, except in high wind. At the crack of dawn, up to 100 hot air balloons traverse the whole region, taking tourists on an extraordinary visual feast above the rock formations. The same event is just as extraordinary when viewed from the ground too, with the early morning silence only broken by the burst from their gas cylinders.

Soon after leaving Cappadocia there were no tourists in sight. The countryside was still quite beautiful with plenty of well cultivated fields. However, the further east I travelled, the more arid the landscape became. And more mountainous too.
As the two go hand in hand at times, the population changed. There were fewer people and vehicles along the road, and fewer large towns, but in Turkey, more guns. I had become accustomed to seeing police and military in Istanbul with guns, and was quite comfortable with that, but now I started to see more of them. They were larger too. Roadblocks and check-points were more frequent, and often accompanied by machine gun installations. As well as heading towards Iran, I was also heading nearer to Iraq and Syria. Perhaps a little naively I saw the guns as security for me. They were there to protect the population, and that included me for a while. Nights in Sivas and Erzurum were uneventful, but Dogubayazit had a different feel to it. It is in the extreme east of Turkey, and close to my planned border entry point into Iran. Most Turkish people had greeted me cordially and with something of a smile up until now, but this town felt different. As I entered it I sheltered from a hailstorm in a petrol station forecourt. The locals looked at me sternly, even frowning, but eventually I think they might have realised that the stranger in their midst was not a threat to them, and in due course started to ask me the usual questions about my bike. They directed me

to my hotel for which I was grateful as my satellite navigation system had nothing recorded for this part of the world. A Spanish number plate on an adventure bike in the scruff of land opposite the hotel was comforting. I later met up with Jose who kindly shared his last packet of Iberico ham with me. The day before he had ridden a little too close to to the Syria border where soldiers had little difficulty in communicating the dangers ahead to him. He heard the sounds of war and turned back.

There was only one street in Dogubayazit with a choice of restaurants, but all had the same menu. There were three choices on each menu; chicken kebabs, lamb kebabs or kebabs with chicken and lamb. I was staying for three nights so that was enough choice for me.

I am not overly familiar with the sound of gunfire, but awoke early the next day to what I assumed to be the sound of it. I counted six shots and was certain that they had been fired extremely close to the hotel. I also heard screams followed by the sound of emergency sirens. At breakfast I spoke to Billal the proprietor, who could manage a basic conversation in English. He said he heard gunfire too, but assumed it was of no particular consequence, as it was a common occurrence. He explained that guns are easy enough to own here, as many have slipped out of police and army ownership into private hands. By the evening he had found out what had happened. In a side street to the hotel, just around the first corner, a simple argument had broken out between children from two particular families. This escalated when the adolescents from the families arrived. One of them pulled out a pistol, shot three dead, and seriously injured two others. The youth was immediately caught and could expect to be given an eighteen year sentence.

I wasn't able to relax in Dogubayazit but instead focused my thoughts on the journey ahead in Iran. I was due to meet my guide at the border crossing in a couple of day's time. In the meantime I headed out of town to Mount Ararat. It didn't look quite like those childhood images I had seen in the book of Genesis in the Old Testament. If Noah had landed his Arc on this one he would have rolled over sideways. Nevertheless I was pleased to have seen it. It is quite different to other mountains, and claims to be the world largest single mountain cone, measured by its base circumference. It is isolated from any other mountain, not in a range, and close enough to the rivers Tigris and Euphrates to imagine flooded plains subsiding to reveal Mount Ararat before other peaks. However the mountain was not named as Noah's landing place until the mid 13th. Century by a Franciscan missionary, and even then some mis-translations may have led to assumptions. However, he had to have landed somewhere so this was as good a place as any for me.

I also visited the Ishak Pasha Palace. It is a beautiful Ottoman construction dating back to 1685, well located if a little remote, and was once an administrative centre of power in the Beyazit province. Although interesting, it did little to help me overcome a certain feeling of discomfort with my time in east Turkey.

After passing through several fortified army check points, a substantial line of trucks eventually appeared, indicating that I must be nearing the frontier, and gateway to Iran. I had no way of determining what was in the trucks, but raised a wry smile to myself wondering how effective the worldwide trade embargo with Iran was working. At the head of the line there were colossal banners with images of Ayatollah Khomeini and Ayatollah Khamenei. I parked my bike in front of a gate and headed by foot through the passport door. It took me a while to pick up on the fact that nobody but me was waiting patiently in line like an Englishman, so I joined the scrum and received a few thumbs up from others for getting the hang of it at last. I got in, and was taken to another office to process my bike documents. A quite attractive lady, clothed in Hijab but with a western smile, asked me for my Carnet. I replied that I didn't have one, and asked to buy one here. Her reply was not entirely without surprise, but still not what I wanted to hear. "We do not sell Carnets here. You can buy one in London."

I recalled my previous decision to work out border restrictions as I went along, having been confused by on-line information about on-going Carnet acceptance around the world. I had a problem to solve, and smiling alone was not going to solve it.

I explained that my official guide, who was obliged to escort me at all times, would be waiting for me by now, the other side of the gate. I was escorted to him. The charming Aydin Nezafat remained calm as I recounted the situation, and arranged for us to meet the senior officer. His office was spacious compared to the world outside of his door. There was plenty of room for him, his over-sized desk and chair, immaculate uniform plastered with braid, golden epaulettes and two rows of medals, and us. He quickly realised that my passport had its Iran arrival stamp in it, with my 10 day visa now counting down, but my bike was the wrong side of his front gate. With reluctance he said there was a way to buy a visa from a service that was still officially approved, but that his country was rapidly moving away from permitting this, in favour of using the Carnet de Passage en Douane system. I met the Iran Carnet agent, and agreed the price he asked. I had no choice. We could not conclude things there and then, but had to return first thing the following morning to do so. Aydin drove to a hotel, and we enjoyed a meal together whilst getting to know each other. He had been introduced to me by the visa agent in the UK. Normally he would escort small groups of visitors but my solo voyage on a motorcycle was not a unique experience for him. It transpired that he was a leading light in the Iran Tour Guide Association, and had recently organised a conference in Iran with representatives from seventy countries from around the world. Aydin also took me to a currency exchange business. Iran is excluded from the International banking system and therefore foreign credit cards are not accepted. At least I knew this to be the case before I arrived, and had some US dollars stuffed around the bike. The money exchanger was quite shocked to learn that I was from the UK, and asked: "Why do you want to visit Iran when you hate us so much?". I took a step back. "I don't hate you at all. I'm here to enjoy your country and study its culture and history. I have several Iranian friends in London. Perhaps our governments are not best friends, but I am here with love in my heart." He almost managed a smile.

The following day we caught up with the Carnet man at the border. All was in order to proceed, but the day before he had in fact not seen my bike. Once he saw the size his eyes lit up and without hesitation demanded a further US$100 from me. I refused and a shouting match followed. I argued that we shook hands yesterday, and a handshake is a man's bond. I stood my ground as he continued to reference the size of the bike, although acknowledging that it still only had two wheels and was indeed a motorcycle. In due course, I agreed a small extra payment, on Aydin's advice, and started my ride in Iran.

Even before we passed through the first town, people had started to stare and wave at me. Much like the man at the border, it was the sheer size of the Rocket that was attracting so much attention. Iranians were not allowed to own a bike larger than 200cc, all of them assembled or built in Iran. Foreigners are permitted to pass through on larger bikes, and I assumed that they were aware of other bikes outside Iran, but nevertheless their reaction seemed overly exuberant. Many waved me to stop so that they could take a photograph. That wasn't always possible, but if I could, I would. Stopping for fuel or refreshments was also an extraordinary experience. After taking my photo, people would offer me a sweet, or a drink, or some fruit. They would also offer to share their picnic meal with me. Iranians are exceptional picnicers. Along every major road around the middle of the day they would lay out a cloth on the ground, preferably on grass, and enjoy a family picnic. Roundabouts were a favourite spot, because they generally featured a thicker carpet of cultivated grass.

At the first army check point I was pulled over. Aydin drove on but stopped a hundred metres further ahead. I tried to gesture that I was following my guide, as four of them, heavily armed, walked around my bike. They didn't ask to see my papers, but shouted a few things at the open office door nearby. The expression that I had become used to on my journey was now evident on their faces. They weren't interested in me at all, just the bike. They all whipped out their phones and quickly took photos before the boss in the office made an appearance and they scuttled away with a smile. It seemed that my presence alone in their country, on my Rocket, was enough to make their day. An entirely unexpected consequence to my ride through Iran was starting to emerge. A moment shared with me seemed to delight them. "Where are you from?" they would all ask. "Inglestan" I learnt was to be my reply. I tried to stay as long as I dared to see their smile, and always left with a smile myself.

I managed to follow Aydin easily enough into the centre of Tabriz for the first night of my schedule. My chosen route through Iran was to be no longer than 10 days. This not only complied with my visa stipulation, but was also kept the cost of employing Aydin to a minimum. As I was a group of one, not ten people, I was paying his entire fee as well as expenses. Tabriz was his home town so he would stay with his family that night, and checked me in to a hotel. After changing out of my leathers, we set off to see my first UNESCO World Heritage Site in his country.

He told me with considerable pride that UNESCO (United Nations Educational, Scientific and Cultural Organisation) had just agreed to protect its 22nd. World Heritage Site in Iran. I had no idea there were so many. It is now the 10th. most numerous country in the world.

As we approached the Blue Mosque Aydin explained that it was built in 1465, but had been almost completely destroyed by an earthquake in 1780. Rebuilding had been a lengthy, painstaking process, as its walls were not covered by tiles, but by mosaic. Every little piece of the deep blue stones that could be recovered had been perfectly repositioned, repeating the incredible workmanship that went into the original construction. As the original local blue stone mine was now depleted, a lighter shade had been used to fill in the gaps. It also highlighted the difference between old and new but both were staggering beautiful. The supporting ancient brickwork, including an arched gallery, also reveals the remarkable care that has been taken.

Tabriz continued to fascinate me. It has a long history, with many significant political and cultural changes over the years. The fact that the historic Silk Road runs through the middle of it has contributed to many of those changes. Marco Polo passed through here, and now it was my turn.

The covered bazaar is the largest in the world, spreading out even further than the Grand Bazaar in Istanbul. It is also one of the oldest in the middle east, remaining an important centre for commodities and cultural exchange. Many intersections feature domed ceilings beautifully constructed in fine brickwork. I visited the carpet specialist area, called Mozzafarieh, and enjoyed a cup of tea and warm greetings from passers by.

The temperature rose the following day as we headed south, hitting a hefty 40°C. approaching Tehran. Along the main roads I was getting used to driving practices. In fact Turkey had taught me quite a lot about how to avoid an accident, and Iran drivers even more so. They follow international standards well enough, but seem to have another set of unwritten rules for themselves. Basically it was my responsibility to avoid them hitting me, not theirs. If they were beside or in front of me, they had a right to drive as they wanted. Crossing my path and then braking in front of me was common practice. On the main roads I was often overtaken by cars who then rapidly braked to slow down, leaving me to ride past them again to keep up with Aydin ahead. On the first few occasions that this happened I would turn my head towards my driver preparing to offer a typically European scowl towards them. However, the scowl was unnecessary but a smile and wave was what was needed. Everybody in the car, driver and passengers, had their phone in their hands and were photographing and videoing me as I rode past. A few of them repeated the drive past and brake procedure to get a better view. Even riding at speed I became comfortable with the routine and obliged whenever possible. I later decided that, without exaggeration, I was probably photographed over 100 times a day in Iran.

The camera-phone operation gathered pace as we entered the outskirts of the capital. One young man on a motorbike stopped at lights to welcome me. He spoke English and after a couple of quick questions, now riding along beside me, he asked for my Instagram address. We stopped but the lights changed again as I answered. That didn't stop him. With his right hand on the throttle, and his left around his phone, he typed my address with his thumb, whilst continuing to fire questions at me. Crazy or skillful, I couldn't decide.

We reached a hotel with both the bike and me sweating profusely. Some of the water coolant boiled out of the reservoir and produced a small puddle on the ground. This was a first for the Rocket, clearly telling me it had reached a new limit. 40°C. was a limit for me too, in leathers.

Tehran was a huge, sprawling city, with many districts. We took the Metro, with its male / female segregated carriages, to north Tehran. Another mosque, but this one also took my breath away. Inside, the multi-roomed Imāmzādeh Sāleh mausoleum is covered in a mirror mosaic, reflecting light but not your own image. Apparently I was allowed to call it 'bling', but preferred to respect its unique atmosphere. In the plaza in front of the mosque clerics and worshipers gathered in the early evening light. The atmosphere was warm and busy with a slight aroma of unwashed bodies. Overhead lighting strung from the minarets led my eyes down to an electronic billboard. It featured an image of a line of bodybags, reminding everybody that a 1988 scheduled passenger plane was shot down by a US missile over Iran territory. A tragic error that somebody did not want to be forgotten. The text read: "Down with USA and Israel".

In fact the same slogan was repeated around the city. Modest sized posters are attached to the railings on the former US Embassy, where fifty two diplomats were held hostage for four hundred and forty four days between 1979 and 1981. Larger drapes featuring Donald Trump line a boulevard. One in particular caught my eye as it showed him in caricature dressed as Adolf Hitler.

Next stop, in the centre of the country, was Isfahan. It was the capital of Persia for several centuries, and continues to take advantage of its location in modern-day Iran. It was described as "half the world" as so much had been going on there.

The magnificent central space called Naghsh-e Jahan Square, which used to be a Polo field, is lined with Persian-Islamic architecture. A two story row of shops is bursting with an extraordinary range of crafts.

The Shah Mosque, or Friday mosque as it was known, again took my breath away. The blue tile adorned building included the most perfectly acoustic dome. A clap softly echoes twenty-four times. The exquisite tile pattern matches many of the local carpets for sale. I understood they still debate whether carpet weavers copied the mosque, or vice-versa. In any event the carpets have seventy silk stitches per centimetre to match the pattern.

There was also a female only mosque, a Palace, a lake, and fountains. Thousands of people enjoyed pic-nics, games, and each others' company every evening, and created a fabulous atmosphere.

Further south, the 2500 year old Persepolis had long since captured my imagination. Built over a period of years by Shahs of Persia, it was started by Darius I of the Archaemenid Empire. It was later sacked by Alexander the Great, but many of the reliefs are still evident. They tell of the symbolic importance of the bull, lion and griffin, and of how visitors processed through the Palace to deliver gifts to the king. I have to confess to being slightly disappointed by what I saw. This particular world heritage site was not in use for very long, and not that important. The 'famous' reliefs were not so remarkable either. I had seen better in the worlds of ancient Egypt, Greece and Rome. I also learnt of the extravagant 2,500 year celebration of the Persian Empire held here in 1971. It was probably a trigger for a series of events that led to the revolution which deposed the Shah in 1979. As always I was pleased I had gone and could not have drawn my own conclusion without doing so.

Persepolis is near Shiraz, where the grape of the same name was first grown. It still was, but no longer to produce wine. However, in a restaurant there I was amused when a fellow diner crossed the floor to offer me alcohol. Speaking good English he said he knew me to be a foreigner and was probably used to drinking alcohol at meal times. He had some in the boot of his car. I thanked him but declined, and later learnt that alcohol could be bought in Iran after all, but was strictly consumed with friends behind closed doors.

After 1500 miles in Iran we reached the southern port of Bandar Abbas, where the temperature once again topped 40 °C., and now with 80% humidity.

Aydin completed his duties, and fulfilled them well. I had one day to myself here, before hopping over by ferry to Dubai.

However, there were two important tasks to be completed. The first was to rendezvous with a colleague of the Carnet man at the Turkish border, pay some more fees, and confirm that my bike had left Iran. The second was to receive delivery of the new Carnet de Passage en Douane that I had subsequently ordered, with express delivery, from a company in England called CARS. Their response to my predicament had been excellent. With cordial efficiency and a genuine desire help me, they completed my application and sent it to a particular luxury hotel in Bandar Abbas that Aydin felt sure would accept it, even though I was not staying there. I bought a twenty-five page Carnet which I felt would be more than enough to cover all the countries ahead that still used it. I had established with certainty that was to be the next two: Dubai, then India.

The last day dawned. My Iran visa would run out at midnight so I had to leave. But my bike could not get into Dubai without the Carnet. I had tracked the courier service from the UK. It was in Shiraz the day before so I decided to wait at the hotel where it was due to arrive. Nervously I enquired at the front desk, but was horrified to learn that the courier had already attempted his delivery, but was rejected as I had not been staying there. For the first time this week, Aydin's advice had been wrong, and he was now hurtling back up the country to Tabriz.

I put on my best forlorn, please help me face. The Front Office Manager arrived and said she would try and contact the courier for me. She succeeded. I spent the next hour in her delightful company, enjoying one of the most fabulous pot's of tea I can every recall drinking. It was an infusion of Persian rose petals and borage flowers, with just a touch of coriander. The tea, her company, and the arrival of my Carnet revived me.

I shall cherish the memory of Iranian hospitality forever. Their smile, their gifts of sweets, fruit, and tea touched me in a way I had never previously experienced in a country. I had never felt so much joy, so much love, from anywhere else I had ever visited.

In total the port procedures took six hot hours in Bandar Abbas, and remarkably six hot hours again in Sharjah, UAE. In between the two I took an overnight ferry, wedging my bike in amongst about a hundred refrigerated food trailers, and accompanied by no more than fifty foot passengers.

Dubai bedazzled me slightly. After Turkey then Iran it felt too civilised. Good clean roads, gleaming tower blocks, surgical shopping malls, English spoken and American coffee. The only commonality was the vicious summer heat. Parts of the city felt ghostly with just a few expat locals, and even fewer tourists here. Only the Emirati seemed ambivalent to the temperature.

I had a service and tyre change booked with Duseja Triumph, who took excellent care of me. My special edition Rocket X is numbered 190 out of 500. All bear their number on a side panel, and X owners introduce themselves to each other by reference to that number. I was thrilled to see number 500 at Duseja, in for a service too. There weren't too many bikes in Dubai as there really wasn't anywhere to go. Riding straight desert roads, over a dry tight mountain section, and back again is about all you could do. However, meeting like-minded friends in a cafe adds a great deal to the fun. I visited Cafe Rider, bearing similarities to the Bike Shed in London, whilst waiting for Duseja to finish off.

The following day I dropped my bike off for its first wooden crate fitting, then sea container experience. All ran to schedule so I settled in to a further week in Dubai, and allowed a further week in Mumbai, India for it to complete its two week journey.

The air conditioned shopping malls, automated Metro, ski slope with real snow, Burj Khalifa, Burj Al Arab and Atlantis all did their best to entertain me, but in truth my mind was very much still on Dalila. We had done our best to keep things going in recent weeks, despite gaps in connectivity, but what happened next took me by surprise, and plunged me in to despair. She sent me a long message, written with care, full of love in her heart, but ending in *'au revoir.'* The fact that I was riding around the world having so much fun, and would be doing so for at least another year, whilst she was sat at home waiting for me, was too much for her to bear.

5. Lord Ganesha.

Just before leaving London, my dear friend Diana gave me a tiny statue of the Hindu God Lord Ganesha. Also known as Ganpati, he's the one with an elephant's head and a cheeky smile. She chose it for me because he is the God of New Beginnings. He had done his job incredibly well for me so far.

After the death of my wife, and the demise of our company, I certainly needed a new beginning. I opened my heart and my soul and offered it to the world. Even during the first month of my trip I met people who have remained friends, following my journey, and offering me regular encouragement and friendship. Almost daily I met new and fascinating people; the benefit of solo travel. As I have no means of cooking food myself, I take every meal in a cafe or restaurant. I sit down, on my own as always, and look around. Some remarkable conversations have followed; all of them 'new beginnings.'

Lord Ganesha is also an obstacle remover and he has certainly been successful for me here too. Any journey like mine, or even a mini-adventure weekend away, will throw up problems. I am a firm believer that for every problem there is a solution. Some solutions are more difficult to find though. Riding through Europe and Turkey presented few significant problems but failure to secure permission to enter Iran was definitely a substantial obstacle facing me ahead. I applied for permission to apply for a Visa four months before I reached Istanbul. A request for more information about me in the meantime was the only evidence of any kind of progress. So, I needed to work on a Plan B. This would either involve a substantial re-routing of my journey to the north, missing India and Indonesia, or a substantial series of sea passages from Turkey to India. Too much sea for a road trip. Out of the blue, the Ministry of Foreign Affaires in Iran gave their permission. Lord Ganesha, did this have anything to do with you?

In late July 2017 I arrived in Mumbai waiting for my Triumph Rocket X to be released from the port. I was seeing Lord Ganesha everywhere. He was in shop windows, on posters, and

in workshops coming out of three metre high moulds. I saw someone making small shrines for him out of old pallets. They were sold for people to put in their homes, with their statue of Lord Ganesha, and displayed together with flowers, incense and offerings. I suddenly realised to my embarrassment, that this little chap was incredibly important to Hindus. The number of people living below the poverty line had diminished thanks to India's healthy growth in recent years, but it was still over 150 million. I stopped to consider how hard the Hindu's amongst this number must pray to Lord Ganesha every day for a new beginning. They needed it more than I did that's for sure.
Having said that, I wanted Lord Ganesha on my side once again. I needed my new beginning to continue safely. From what I saw on the roads, and everything I learnt before I arrived, I realised I was going to have to ask him to do his best for me. India's roads were truly awful. Potholes, cracked concrete, sections of missing tarmac even on toll roads, no lines to follow, no junction markings, few road signs, huge speed bumps placed at random, and the list went on. The drivers were even worse. Trucks, cars, bikes, taxis and rickshaws all seemed to have their individual set of rules. The blast of a horn had at least a dozen meanings, including "I'm about to turn right across your path even though I can see you coming up beside me, so here's a blast of my horn instead of using my indicator, which I don't know how to use anyway". I didn't know how to pray to Lord Ganesha, but if I did, I would have.

Mumbai was a colossal culture shock for me, more so than anywhere I had ever been before. Busy, noisy, smelly, and dirty was well within my range of expectations, but the poverty made me wretch. The road from the airport followed a railway line, a sewer, and a continuous row of people living on the street. Someone tried to convince me they were economic migrants, not homeless, but all I could see was desperation in their eyes. Tree branches and sticks held a filthy canvas over their heads to make a shelter. A pot over a single flame was in the opening, and food, probably only vegetables, was prepared on the ground. Men urinated freely on the street, and women squatted behind the odd tree. Public toilet blocks were in evidence a little nearer the middle of the city, but I dreaded to think what they might have been like inside. Between these squats were piles of rancid rubbish, with a stench beyond my ability to adequately describe. My hotel was clean enough, and served some very tasty food. Whilst I busied myself being a tourist for a few days, waiting for news of my bike's arrival, I was utterly dismayed to learn that the number one tourist attraction in Mumbai was the slums. I would be so ashamed if that was said of my home city, but the popularity of the film "Slumdog Millionaire" had sent more people flocking to see them. Good for business then. I had to go and judge for myself.

My young guide took me first to the laundry. Up to one hundred men and women wash people's clothes by hand here, rubbing and thrashing them with soap and water, standing in and bending over concrete tubs to do so. Other groups worked their home made washing machines. Large drums, hand beaten in to shape, are rotated back and forwards by a series of belts attached to a huge motor. Soapy water splashes everywhere. Every single item has a cloth tab pinned to it, unique to each client. I was impressed by the efficiency of it all.

Spotting a couple of well dressed children, he then took me to a school, and later to two more. All the classrooms were packed with attentive, uniformed, clean and healthy looking youngsters. Regrettably, everything else I saw was miserable. 80% of the activity in a slum is commercial. They recycle anything and everything from plastic bottles to computers, paint tins to cables, broken pallets to car parts. One workshop had a dozen men crouched over furnaces smelting broken aluminium parts into ingots. I asked my guide if they knew that cyanide is given off in this process. He shook his head, and explained that all of them received no education, and do not know that their life expectancy is only half that of others. Another workshop converted flat leather into fake crocodile skin for handbags and shoes. At the end of their working day, most of the factory workers would cook a meal, then sleep, on the same factory floor.

A substantial proportion of Mumbai's population lived in slums. The actual figure, and even the description of a slum, seemed to vary quite a bit. My guide explained to me that his family had lived in one whilst his father was training to be a doctor. After qualifying they were able to move out.

I moved out too, to an area north of the centre, but still well within the city. There I was able to visit both a freight forwarder and a shipping agent to pay some fees, as well as to visit Triumph Mumbai for a photo opportunity. I was warmly welcomed at Triumph, but the commercial encounters gave me an early insight into India's bureaucracy. They also demanded payments in cash which had me making daily visits to ATMs to circumvent India's low daily withdrawal limit. Great efforts had been made by the government in recent years to suppress the 'cash economy', and limiting cash withdrawals was one of them.

I was ferried from one office to the other on the back of a bike, with no leathers and no helmet, totally against my own rules. I didn't give Lord Ganesha a thought at that moment but instead shrugged my shoulders and got on with it, as countless millions of Indians do every day. It was not until a while later I read that an average of three Mumbai motorcyclists are killed every day as a direct result of hitting potholes. There are about a dozen more motorcycle fatalities for other reasons. Life in India seemed to be cheap.

I moved on again. This time to the container port on the far side of the bay. There was only one hotel anywhere near the customs office I had to visit so I booked it. I immediately wish I hadn't, and was not consoled by the fact that I had no choice. From about twenty miles away the road was under construction, looking as if it had been in this state for years, with no end in sight. The taxi bounced, rattled and slid along, choking in dust beside an endless stream of sea containers on trucks. My hotel was in a similar state as the road, with a crudely constructed footbridge over a rain water canal to reach it. The canal was also an open sewer. The room I was given had a spectacular view over the back yard of the hotel, which also doubled as a rubbish pit for all the adjoining buildings. The sheets were grey, the wallpaper peeling, and the window was about three inches too small for the frame. The kitchen was filthy - I wish I hadn't looked in - but somehow produced tasty food.

After seven consecutive pre-arranged daily visits to my agent and the Customs House, as well as further visits to the only ATM in town that worked, I was finally reunited with my bike. However, the bureaucratic process got the better of me after the fourth day. I thumped the table and screamed as I realised that a further 24 hours delay had been caused by a lost comma. Leaving Dubai my cargo was described as 'Motorcycle, tools and camping equipment'. In Mumbai it had been described as 'Motorcycle tools and camping equipment'. A Customs Officer demanded to know where the motorcycle had gone to.

After a week in the most disgusting excuse for a hotel I had ever imagined might exist, a week of mind numbing bureaucracy, a week of filth everywhere, a week of almost non-functioning internet and ATMs, as well as incessant noise, I was beginning to come to an interesting conclusion. If I stopped fighting India I might get more out of it. Instead of thinking that nothing was working properly, I should accept that it works for 1.3 billion Indians, and go with the flow. Surely they couldn't all be wrong. It was me that was wrong. Everyone I had met so far accepted everything with good grace. It was their lives, their culture, and their country. On my first day on the road, two things confirmed to me I needed to accept that change. Scarcely a mile after leaving the hotel the road construction team diverted everybody off the road, but failed to divert us all back on it. I followed the belching traffic for another mile down a dirt track laughing inside my helmet as I realised that this, today, was how all of Mumbai's port traffic was going to enter the country's road network. Eventually we crossed a railway track, unmanned and unpaved, bouncing uncontrollably over the lines, before rejoining the main road, still within the construction area. It was a solution to the problem of half a diversion. Just like all the little problems in India, everybody just gets on with finding a solution. Riding on, I got lost three times trying to leave Mumbai on the main road north. My Satellite Navigation system did not work. After buying the map online whilst in Dubai, and getting very frustrated by its failure to download, Tom Tom eventually told me that they didn't have a map for their motorcycle 'Rider' product in India. Insufficient demand to buy it, I concluded. The paper road atlas I bought was useless, so I had to stop and check my position on my iPhone. It overheated and shut down when sitting in the map pocket on my fuel tank, and therefore was kept in my jacket pocket. The process I developed was to check the route ahead, remember it, and ride. That didn't work too well as there were very few road signs to follow. Eventually I pulled across a central reservation to make a u-turn, following others, stopped for a pee, following others, and then stopped at a cafe for lunch. I washed my hands using the basin provided, again following others, ordered a fantastically tasty vegetable thali, drinking cool fresh water from the basin, following others, and eventually realised I had a huge smile on my face. I was getting used to India. I was even starting to like it.

However, many people offered me cautionary advice on the standard of driving here, or lack of a standard, prior to my arrival. However, after Turkey, then Iran, I found that things weren't so bad after all. There was so much traffic everywhere that no-one could travel fast. At low speeds the traffic filtered well with every road user. I learnt more about use of the horn. It could be used to advise others of a turn, an undertake, a get out of my way message, an expression of annoyance, a my turn next message and doubtless many other things that I never figured out. Somehow, incredibly, the system of un-written rules, and ignored legislation, worked well. To my surprise, I even concluded that it worked really well. The bigger the vehicle, the more expensive the vehicle, the more 'rights' you had. Trucks and buses ruled the highways, mini vans and 4 x 4s came next, rare imported cars followed, then Indian made cars, then my motorcycle, then Royal Enfield Bullets, then all other motorcycles, then rickshaws, also known as tuk-tuks, then carts drawn by horse, ox, donkey or camel, then cyclists and pedestrians. Pedestrians walk in the street because the pavements are even worse than the roads, or non existent. But top of the tree by far are the cows. They are holy of course, and hitting one is completely out of the question. I asked several times but never found out what would happen if I hit one. People just said I should not do it. Unlike in Turkey my bike was given a higher status than other motorcycles. It took other road users only a fraction of a second to spot my size and give me a little extra space. That embarrassed me most of the time, but I was very grateful for the allowance. Honestly, I felt quite safe with other users on the roads here. I was also quite comfortable with traffic coming down the street the wrong way towards me. It really all worked well for them, even if they have made up many of the rules for themselves. The secret was to observe what they did, and follow. I would have failed if I tried to impose my knowledge of international traffic laws on to them.

I spent quite some time, on more than one occasion, just staring at a particular road junction close to my second hotel in north Mumbai. Five roads intersected under a railway flyover. The road was not flat and had much of its original surface missing. There were no traffic lights, no roundabouts, no road markings, and no respite to the incessant stream of users. Everyone just filtered through, one after the other, usually in small groups. Buses charged, cars hesitated, slightly, pedestrians didn't. Rickshaws got in everyone's way, and motorcyclists risked certain injury if they got it wrong. It seemed utterly incredible to me that this could work, but it did.

However, even after just a few days on the road in India I came to an unavoidable conclusion about their roads. They are terrible. Missing tarmac and potholes the size of small craters had plagued me. Explaining why an adequately built toll road can have a ten metre or ten kilometre section of rough shingle but no tarmac eluded me. The towns are the worst. Many had little more than mud in them, and none of that was flat. Most of them had tarmac once, I was told, but after digging up to install or maintain local services, there was no budget left for resurfacing. Probably no votes for the councillors and politicians either. Corruption stories filled the newspapers daily. In my mind peoples' lives were blighted by the disgraceful roads in their towns, but I gained the impression that they were largely ambivalent to it.

Motorcyclists were not charged for using toll roads, but to get past the booths and barriers you had to ride down a very narrow channel on the side of the road. Just after doing so I would often stop at one of the many refreshment shacks. They all served masala chai tea which soon became a favourite of mine. It was India's famous hot, milky, spiced tea. An exotic mix of cardamon, cloves, cinnamon, peppercorns, nutmeg and ginger are added to a tea and milk mix, then boiled and sieved before serving in a small cup. Approaching Modasa, north of Mumbai, I met Ravi Patel over a cup of masala chai. He and his small group of friends asked me about my journey, and listened attentively to my responses. After explaining that he was a journalist I was happy to agree to him writing about me. I saw the article later, but of course it was written in Hindi. I think he focused on my 'please stop smoking' message. That article led to two further regional newspaper articles, and a television interview. I was famous for a day in Gujurat.

The first stop on my tour of India's "Golden Triangle" was Udaipur. It is known as the "City of Lakes". Five man-made lakes provide fresh water for the inhabitants and allowed the city to flourish as a regional capital. They now made a charming backdrop for tourists, with fabulous palaces and a fort along their banks. One palace in the middle of a lake is now a much photographed luxury hotel. There is also a terrific Hindu temple called Jagdish right in the busy heart of the city.
From my third floor hotel bedroom window I watched small groups of people arrive on some steps on the edge of Lake Pichola just below me. With the water level covering their modesty, they removed their clothes, washed themselves with generous amounts of soap, then washed their clothes and put them back on again, whilst still in the lake. The ladies area was discreetly away from the mens area, but I was able to observe their well rehearsed process with equal discretion and considerable dexterity. Putting a sari on in the water was quite a challenge.

I lost my way again trying to find the main road from Udaipur to Jodhpur. With just my phone in my pocket, I was also having to stop and ask locals for directions. Unfortunately their contribution was not adding anything useful to my predicament. Their hand gestures were loose and imprecise, at least to my understanding. On a dirt road through some hills I stopped at a cafe. It had some painted concrete blocks for walls, a tin and plastic roof, a few stools on the ground, and served a delicious cup of masala chai tea. I ordered a freshly cooked vegetable samosa which by now had also become a favourite snack. But the highlight of this stop was the two children who played excitedly around my bike long enough for me to invite their father to lift them on to the seat for a photograph. It became a favourite shot from India. So too was the photo of a very attractive young lady who stopped to admire my bike, just after I had ridden past, admiring her. She was riding a Royal Enfield Bullet; her husband was the pillion. I stopped to check directions but a great conversation followed instead, as well as an exchange of photos. Later on I met a lively crowd of young Hindus on a pilgrimage. The impromptu photo of them managed to capture the magic of that little moment too.

Festivals in India seem to happen on a regular basis. I eventually arrived in Jodhpur right in the middle of one. Large crowds, blocked streets, and fireworks brought a smile to my face, but didn't help me find my hotel in the centre of the old town. Like so many, Jodhpur had a historic centre, walled at one time, but now enveloped by modern industry. To correct for a series of errors I found myself riding through the middle of their celebration, on a street only wide enough for rickshaws, bikes and pedestrians, explaining my ineptitude with a very English "Hello" as they parted a way for me.

Jodhpur boomed in the days of the Raj who built many forts, palaces and temples. Towering over the city on a rocky hill is the magnificent and very well fortified Mehrangarh 'red' fort. Despite its principal defence purpose, it featured intricate carvings and opulent courtyards. Below it, the so-called 'blue' city intrigued me. Houses were once painted blue in this district to indicate that the occupants were Brahmins, India's highest cast. From a distance they looked attractive, but up close, they were mostly scruffy, dirty, mouldy and needed re-painting. I decided that either the Brahmins had moved out, or had fallen on hard times, or the blue paint salesman had retired.

Being a tourist in Jodhpur is hungry work so frequent stops for more freshly cooked vegetable samosas, this time served with a mint and coriander dip, kept me going. A poor excuse really; I just liked them. Stepping to the side of a street to enjoy another one, I was spotted by a Dutch family of four. They were more adventurous than most and loved to experience life with a sense of awe. They had just spent a week trekking in north India and the father was about to step into a barber shop to have his first shave in a while, this time with a cut throat razor. I joked about having his throat cut as we parted. A few days later in Jaipur, they drove past me in a mini-van, with the side door open, and the father gesturing a throat cutting movement accompanied by a thumbs up. He had survived, and I think he tried to tell me he had enjoyed the experience.

A different colour this time, Jaipur is known as the Pink City, as many of the buildings in the central area are made from pink sandstone. Others are painted pink. A palace complex called Jantar Mantar was an architectural and cultural feast for me. The intriguing five story 'Palace of Winds' called Hawa Mahal is like a honeycomb with hundreds of small windows and intricate latticework.

Walks around the town and more cups of masala chai were also delightful. I stopped to admire another unfathomable element of Indian life. In a busy street, wedged between a clothes shop selling colourful saris, and an electronics store, was an open-fronted shop selling used railway tracks. The space was full of them. A sour-faced man sat on top of the pile, presumably waiting for a customer.

I took a rickshaw ride one afternoon in heavy traffic. Walking in the opposite direction to me, nonchalantly strolling down the street without a care in the world, was an elephant. She was to the side of the road, unaccompanied, heading for the shops with a shopping list. "Twenty kilos of fresh green branches, and a couple of your finest vegetable samosas please", I imagined.

I was in fact heading out to visit an elephant sanctuary. I learnt that the old lady left the complex every afternoon for her walk, returning an hour or so later. Everybody knew her, and were as content as she was to take a daily stroll. Other elephants in the complex were a little infirm due to maltreatment, and some were even grumpy. It was a private sanctuary, and needed more resources.

Leaving Jaipur I was waived down for a photo, and happily obliged. It turned out be a mammoth photo session with a succession of men mounting my bike for their friends to take a shot. A few minutes later I had to call a halt after realising I had blocked both sides of a two lane artery with everybody stopping to see what was happening. Oops.

Next stop was the romance of The Taj Mahal.

But romance was already in the air for me.

Heading over Tower Bridge, London, then west to Ireland.

Decide for yourself if Dalila's huge smile is for me or my bike.

Istanbul, Turkey. Goodbye Europe, hello Asia.

Military checkpoint, east Turkey.

Taking tea on the silk road in Tabriz, Iran.

Blue Mosque, Isfahan, Iran.

Laundry service in a Mumbai slum, India.

Whose road is it?

Another little moment of magic in India.

Exquisite. The Taj Mahal, India.

View of Mount Everest, Nepal, from Kala Patthar.

Angkor Wat, Cambodia.

6. Love, loss, and love again.

After Dalila's "Au revoir" letter I too reflected on the sensibility of keeping a relationship in France going whilst I still had over a year of my journey ahead. We had previously talked before about how difficult it was. I recognised that it was probably more difficult for her than me. As she pointed out, I was having a lot of fun riding around the world whilst she was sat at home in Lyon, declining invitations that she might otherwise have accepted. However, I also knew there was more to her malaise than she had written about. One of her sisters had died earlier in the year. All the family were in shock, and Dalila absorbed much of their grief. Perhaps a little later than the others, it had started to have a deeper impact on her. Furthermore, she was having difficulties with an aspect of her work.

Despite the complication of distance, I felt sure that the emotional connection was strong enough to win through.

Two days after I received her email, I wrote back. I spoke about her sister, and her work, and encouraged her to talk more to me about those issues. I made it clear that I wanted to help her, but couldn't do so if I was not part of her life. I think she smiled, her heart filled, and she wrote back. I listened and supported as she opened up to me. My heart filled too, as I realised we had found the right words to keep going. The WhatsApp conversations continued, and accelerated.

It was time to visit The Taj Mahal. There are places you look forward to going to which disappoint, and there are places which exceed your expectations. The danger with dreaming about visiting a classic for as long as you can remember, is that the risk of disappointment increases. However, The Taj Mahal surpassed my expectations by a very long way. It was the most beautiful building I had ever seen. Emotions tugged in every direction. The setting on the south bank of the Yamuna River, its glorious design, remarkable craftsmanship, exceptional material selection, and dedication to love and loss, are all perfect. It was so gorgeous.

'Exquisite' was the best single word description I could conjure up to describe The Taj Mahal, but it was hopelessly inadequate really. It was built as a mausoleum by Mughal emperor Shah Jahan between 1632 and 1643 to house the tomb of his favourite wife Mumtaz Mahal. She died giving birth to their fourteenth child. The ivory white marble, sourced from all over India, still looked pristine today. Famously it reflected the colour of the early morning sun, so that was the time of day I decided to go. The craftsmanship was also overwhelming. Black marble is inlaid throughout. So too were the beautifully soft and swirling arabesque letters, depicting passages from the Quran. Semi-precious stones were originally a feature of the building but all have been subsequently stolen. Thanks go to Lord Curzon in the mid nineteenth century for his decision to renovate where needed and upgrade the garden layout, especially the two lakes. They reflect the shape of the building and enhance your wonderment as you enter the site through an arched gateway.

I was the very first person in through the gates that day; my reward for getting up at 4.30am. A guide rushed me around to the best photograph locations before anyone else got there. It was a real privilege. I later strolled around slowly, sitting and staring in awe.

The four minarets lean outwards, slightly. That's deliberate so that should they fall in an earthquake they will not damage the mausoleum. Apparently there was a plan to build a 'double' on the opposite bank of the Yamuna River, in black marble. Time and events overtook the plan but not before much of the marble had been acquired. It is probably only a myth, but I was told that the marble was now in Trafalgar Square, London.

Despite The Taj Mahal attracting over 20,000 visitors a day, I bumped into four people I knew. The dutch family from Jodhpur and Jaipur. We strolled around the mausoleum together, slowly, and for a second time.

The Taj Mahal is included in the "Seven New Wonders of the World 2016" list. And so it should be.

I had been in India for over a month by this point, and so far all ten hotels that I had stayed in now merited inclusion in my list of eleven worst hotels ever. The eleventh was somewhere in Oklahoma, USA a few years before. Many were simply dirty. I didn't know if the dust clung to the humidity everywhere, or the cleaning methods were inadequate. All suffered from power cuts throughout the day. Air conditioning failed even more frequently. Most had very weak wi-fi even though they all promoted the fact that they offered it free of charge. Some had grey bedsheets. One had peeling wallpaper. All had mould in the bathroom. Most had running water, sometimes a touch above tepid. One had just one light fixture working out of five. I often commented on these issues when asked by enthusiastic management, but nothing changed. Heading towards Delhi, the capital, I was hoping for a higher standard.

After a false start I found one. The staff were very considerate and secured my bike in a locked alleyway. It was open to the elements, and in an Indian summer that included high temperatures and humidity. I made the mistake of storing my leathers, boots and helmet in the trunk. They picked up a thick layer of mould very quickly. I managed to get them cleaned well enough, after a bit of an effort, but never got rid of the smell.

Security was particularly important to me as I had now settled on a plan for the next month which involved leaving India by air three times. The first was to catch up with Dalila again.

We settled on meeting up in Malaga, Spain. She had a little time to spare in late August, and I could fly back easily enough. We booked a room in a house tucked behind Marbella. Some very good friends of mine were able to join us in the house for a few days. They were the first to meet Dalila. I asked a family member to join us, but it was still too soon after Sue for them to consider doing so. I respected their decision, and agreed with them.

By now Dalila and I had reached a decision about our future. At the end of my journey I would come and live with her, choosing a new country, a new language, and new friends in the process. Apart from anything else, this would suit me well. After all, I had set off from the UK, with an open mind and open soul, to find something else. I did not know what at the time. I certainly did not expect that 'something' to be a woman. I did have in mind a new country, certainly, and perhaps a new business idea or a job. Lyon appealed to me.

However, that commitment begged another question. We had often discussed our views on marriage, divorce, commitment for life, and religion. Our opinions were identical on every issue. Dalila had never been married before, and we had never discussed the possibility of us marrying. The idea had certainly been circulating under my helmet, and I thought further about it on the plane to Malaga. I was determined not to get carried away though. I kept telling myself that there was no need to even think about it at this stage, let alone talk to her about it. After all, we had only spent just eleven days together up till now, and I still had a long way to ride. The question could certainly wait. It turned out that Dalila had been having exactly the same thoughts. We managed to coincide our arrival at Malaga Airport to within an hour of each other. As we left the terminal building together she asked me:

"Mark, whilst on holiday here, is there a question you are planning to ask me?"

I gritted my teeth, lowered my head, tensed my muscles, but the grin gave it away immediately. I couldn't help myself. I was delighted to hear her question. Ecstatic in fact.

"Yes Darling, there is".

You should have seen our faces. Smiles beamed from ear to ear.

"But the airline has left my suitcase behind and will deliver it to our house tomorrow. Can the question wait until I have some clean clothes?" Of course it could.

The following evening, on just our 12th day together, beside our table in the corner of a cosy restaurant, I went down on one knee. In my best french, with a pounding heart, I asked the question:

"Dalila, à la fin de mon voyage, veux-tu m'épouser?"

("Dalila, at the end of my journey, will you marry me?")

"Oh oui Mark, ouiiiiiiii".
("Oh yes Mark, yeeeees.")

A lovely holiday followed. My friends were thrilled to meet her, and learn our news. We spent the days exploring the Andalusia region enjoying beaches, bars and restaurants, as well as taking in a few of the sights. We also met new friends staying in the same house. The private pool there became a cherished spot for us late at night.
Dalila loves to swim, especially in the sea. We enjoyed just splashing around in the waves too. One of my more childish moments with my family had often been to imitate "Jaws" in the water. I would swim slowly towards my sons with one hand extended above my head, repeating the film score. "da-dan …. da-dan …. da-dan…". Dalila latched on immediately, but gradually increased the speed of the "da-dans". I realised where she was going. Spontaneously, and with perfect synchronisation, changing from the "Jaws" score to the chorus from Frankie Valli's "Can't take my eyes off you". The "da-dans" sped up to "da-dan, da-dan, da-dada-da, I love you baby, and if it's quite alright, I need you baby, to warm the lonely nights, I love you baby, trust in me when I say." We danced around, circling each other, and singing as loud as we could. The moment seemed to confirm our compatibility.

The airport departure was the same as before. Difficult, tearful, and ending in a reminder that I was still going around the world.

7. *"Jum, jum"* to the top of the world.

I returned to my bike in Delhi, but had already made a series of big decisions by the time I got there.
My intended route was to continue across northern India and into Nepal. I would then u-turn back to India and head east through the tea plantations, over the top of Bangladesh, through Myanmar to Thailand, divert to Cambodia for a week, back into Thailand, and south through Malaysia, Singapore and on to Indonesia. As my eldest son and daughter-in-law lived in Indonesia, and especially as they had just produced my first granddaughter, it was imperative that I spent some time with them there.

Late monsoons had flooded and damaged some roads and bridges in both northern India as well as in Nepal. I could wait for better news of the conditions, perhaps, or fly in and out of Nepal from Delhi instead. I also wondered if my ghastly week at Mumbai port, and the fight with Indian bureaucracy, might be repeated when trying to cross back from Nepal into India. I opted to fly. In fact, I was never at any stage determined to ride in Nepal, but my goal was always to get to Kathmandu, then Lukla, and trek to Mount Everest base camp. I couldn't get up Everest with the Rocket anyway. But I thought about it!

After India lay Myanmar. I knew I would need to obtain a visa following a process similar to that of Iran. The first step was to employ a guiding company who in turn were obliged to assign both a guide and a liaison officer to me. I would of course have to pay for their services, as well as their accommodation and travel expenses. The cost was very high, although I still looked forward to seeing some of Myanmar's sights and meeting the people, closed to the world for so many years. However, whilst en route, I learnt that Thailand too was now insisting I employed a guide, not just for myself, but for the fact that I wanted to ride my own vehicle in their country. I couldn't understand why they imposed this regulation, despite asking, and couldn't find a way around it either. The cost was even higher than Myanmar.

Reluctantly, and grumpily, I decided to skip both countries, and ship my bike directly from India to Malaysia.

Leaving India was to be simple enough, employing the Delhi branch of the same company I used to get in to Mumbai. Looking back I have to laugh. India's bureaucracy is utterly amazing. I had to accompany my agent on seven more daily visits to the Customs House in Delhi. Each day made slightly more progress. My bike was crated, then uncrated for serial number inspections, then crated again. The export paperwork now included reference to the fact that it was 'hazardous goods', because of the battery and very nearly completely empty fuel tank. It had entered India as non-hazardous. Now for the authorisation processes. Signatures were needed from an Assistant Commissioner, a Deputy Commissioner, a Joint Commissioner, the Commissioner and finally the Chief Commissioner. At least the waiting lounge in Delhi Customs House was clean. In fact, almost everything in Delhi was cleaner, smarter, and more comfortable than elsewhere. After all, the civil servants and government operate from here.

Whilst I was there the World Bank published it's 'Ease of doing Business Index", country by country. India proudly announced in one of Delhi's newspapers that it had moved up from position 131 to 130 in the world.

My bike's wooden crate could now be popped into a container, and sent by rail back to the west coast, before onward shipping to Kuala Lumpur, Malaysia.

As always, I was researching the road ahead from there. I could enjoy riding around Malaysia for a few days, it is not that large, then hop on to Singapore. I was looking forward to both, even though there is no decent riding to be had on Singapore. Eventually I learnt that this small island does not really want any more vehicles on it, and would charge high fees and service charges to get me both on and off it. Despite that, I knew that I could get a ferry over to an Indonesian island just off shore, and intended to island hop my way to their biggest island, Sumatra, before going on to Java and the capital, Jakarta. However, yet another frustration emerged as I discovered that these ferries are for foot passengers only, not for vehicles or commercial goods.

As a last resort I tried to find 'Mr. Lim and his onion boat'. He had ferried adventure motorcyclists across in the past by craning bikes into his cargo hold, principally taking onions across the Malacca Strait. He had been shut down.

So, reluctantly realising that the world is a more regulated place than it used to be, and that countries want to patrol their borders more rigorously, I was left with no option but to be crated and shipped again in a container to enter Indonesia.

Entering Singapore with no good riding options did not seem worth the expense and effort either. Malaysia looked smaller and smaller every time I looked at a map. The cost of shipping, crating, port charges and so on into Malaysia, out again, and into Indonesia, all began to look very unattractive to me. Eventually I decided to not only forgo riding to Nepal and back, but also to forgo Myanmar, Thailand, Malaysia and Singapore. I diverted my bike's passage out of India directly to Indonesia.

I felt pathetic. I had failed to ride my chosen route. I had compromised too much. The bike was now on a thirty day journey across water when it should have been on land.

In April 2015 a devastating earthquake hit Kathmandu, killing almost 9,000 people in the wider area, and injuring about 22,000 more. The destruction was still clear to see in many places when I arrived although foreign support had poured in. Their small economy is based on agriculture and services, so every little extra from tourism is vital to them. Many of the buildings in the centre of the city had been re-constructed, but the roads, water and electrical services were still needing a great deal of work.

I met up with others who had booked the same trek as me, and we busied ourselves for a couple of days getting acclimatised and kitted out. Motorcyclists don't carry down jackets, walking boots and poles, or large backpacks, so I had to start from scratch.

Famously, the flight from Kathmandu to Lukla ends with an instrument-free, pilot-skills-only landing, on a terrifyingly short uphill strip. Actually I was thrilled by the experience, though others were more nervous. There was a smell of fear in the cabin, signalling that the adventure had really begun.

"*Jum Jum*" said the dragon, and off we went. We just had to put one foot in front of the other, and repeat. Eventually we would get from Lukla to Everest Base Camp. It would only take 8 days. "*Jum Jum*" is Nepalese for "Let's go". Our assistant guide, nineteen year old Draigon, softly uttered these words at the start of every day, as well as after every tea and lunch stop, and indeed after every three minute pause to gasp for air and sip water. Despite his tender age he set the pace really well, taking into account the three 60 year olds in our party of six.

We were all strangers in the Himalayas together, but united by a single goal: Everest. I have often wondered how strangers can get along so well. Our backgrounds, country of origin, culture even, were all so different. Yet we enjoyed the most heartwarming, intimate, and mutually supportive two weeks together. Conversations flowed endlessly and covered every subject - family, friends, love, work, travel, politics and religion. Dawa, our lead guide and sherpa, needed to know at all times how we were feeling, and how our bodies were reacting to the altitude and diet. Consequently, all intimate details were shared.

Fifteen year old Khalil hopped and skipped uphill with a passion and enthusiasm that defied his age, never complaining once. "Would it help if I complained?", he asked. He was a credit to his father who was usually a step or two behind him. Abdul paused to give a wrapped sweet to every other child he passed en route. Generous with all, at the end of the trek he gave us a personalised memento of our time together. Hand carved in Nepalese slate, each bears our name and EBC 17, the local abbreviation for Everest Base Camp, and the year. Praful and I tended to take up the middle of the group. We huffed and puffed and sweated our way along together. Deepa, his daughter and marathon runner, was equally delightful company, and admired for her fitness. My room mate, Chang, was often at the rear, stopping to take the most photographs. He was the joker in the group, cracking comments, one liners, and searching questions to keep us all alert. Dawa took up the rear. "If you see Yaks coming towards you, stick to the inside of the path. They sometimes wobble and might knock you over the edge". We didn't challenge the advice.

Every step has to be taken with care. Uneven steps and occasional flat gravel are welcome passages. More often the path was vertiginous, both up and down. Quads burned, thighs throbbed, knees swelled, toes were crushed, lungs gasped, sweat poured and increasing altitude affected our cognitive ability. It became more and more difficult to think, reason and concentrate. Occasional dizziness and headaches left us all questioning our determination from time to time. An established technique is to climb higher and sleep lower; that may have helped.

The small houses lining the route were simply constructed from wood or stone, with tin roofs. Many had tiny fields beside them, growing root vegetables, but with the odd flower bed. Quite a few of the hamlets had a community room, which to our very great surprise often contained full size snooker tables, always occupied.

The tea houses offering cooked food were really quite good. There were many dishes built around pasta, rice, potatoes or vegetables. A chicken dish or two made an appearance now and then, but otherwise meat was not available. Accommodation was simple with a clean bed but very limited bathroom facilities. Toilets were flushed with a jug of water, basins with a rudimentary flow of water were always communal, and hot showers were a lamentable after-thought. We never complained. Life was very simple for the locals. There was no mains electricity. Solar panels charged large batteries to run dim light bulbs. Bottled gas was carried by porters or yaks for cooking. Wood or peat stoves keep the living space warm at night.

The paths run both uphill and downhill, clinging to the mountainside, almost never allowing a gentle flat respite for a moment. From time to time we had to switch from one side of the Dudhkoshi and Imjakhol rivers to the other. Everybody, yaks and horses included, crossed on the same one metre wide bridges. They are made from tensioned alloy and steel, in quite good condition, mostly, but all allow a full view of the raging torrent way below. They bounced and swung as we made our way to terra firma on the other side, trying to maintain our balance, and hoping to remain ambivalent to the challenge whilst disguising our fear.

Pausing to gaze up at the hills on each side of the valleys, I was struck by their size and beauty as the tree line faded in to the clouds. From time to time the parting mist revealed a sight of unimaginable scale. A white wall, with rocky outcrops, rising like shards to pierce the sky above. The Himalayas are huge!

There are a couple of buddhist monasteries en route with a large one in Tengboche at 3,870 metres. Sharing a celebration with the monks which included rhythmic chanting, simple instruments and incense burning was a humbling experience.

Once the trees and tufts of grass have been left behind, the fearsome rocks lend themselves less suitable for allowing a path to be created. The tail end of the Khumbu glacier then appeared underfoot. It was covered in loose moraine, but we followed the side of it as best we could. The icy broken leading edge of the glacier pushed us away from it slightly, and we lost sight of Everest for a while. Base Camp is empty in September but the grey rocky terrain and the low grey cloud did not dampen the elation of the achievement of being there.

The best view of the summit of Mount Everest, my personal goal, was from Kala Patthar at 5,644 metres. Seeing the top of the world revealed by the rising sun, whilst alone on a side track, brought a flood of emotions. For as long as I could remember I had been fascinated by the mountain. A school visit by the 1953 successful summit ascent expedition leader, Colonel John Hunt, ignited the dream, and becoming a Fellow of the Royal Geographic Society a few years ago, fuelled it. My eyes watered. This was one of the best moments of my life.

The arduous accent was complemented by the speed of the descent, although it still had a number of uphill passages to challenge us. On the last afternoon, Chang was suffering from cramp in his left leg. He was embarrassed by the thought of hiring a horse to complete the trek but eventually conceded that it was the best option. 'Emperor Chang' rode in to town right up to the front door of our final tea house. Warm congratulations were offered to all that night.

Leaving Lukla air strip was even more fun than arriving. We hurtled downhill with all the power available to us, and hoped to be airborne before running out of runway at the cliff edge.

Kathmandu seemed comfortable and familiar after the previous fortnight. I gave my body a rest for a couple of days, and caught up with life beyond the mountains. On consecutive evenings I enjoyed meals in a lively restaurant and met a particularly interesting character. Now a musician living in Melbourne, Australia, he used to be a busker and Norton motorcycle engineer. Phil invited me to stay with him, if ever I got to Melbourne.

8. Hop, skip and jump through Asia.

Returning to Delhi for a few days I was feeling increasingly disappointed with myself for deciding to ship the bike directly to Indonesia. I booked another flight, this time to Siem Reap in Cambodia, but would dearly have loved to have been riding there.

Siem Reap is a burgeoning city, accommodating tourists visiting the Angkor temples. Backpacker hostels, local hotels and international names dominate the centre of the city, with lively bars and restaurants offering anything a man could desire. An endless stream of minders thought that I must be there for sex or drugs, and refused to accept a polite rejection from me as a walked past them. A couple of times I lost my temper and offered them an impolite rejection, but they were hardened to my response. However, I did find myself tempted by one of the local delicacies. A mobile vendor was offering a delicious selection of snacks on a stick. They included fried snake, beetle and some sort of grub. I chose a black scorpion. I couldn't let this probably once in a lifetime opportunity go by, even though it might have been the last thing I did. I crunched away for a few anxious seconds whilst stuffing it all into my mouth before I regretted trying to do so. Some of it went down well enough, but harder parts, the claws I think, were more difficult to swallow. Disappointingly, the only discernible flavour was the frying oil.

I think it must have been Walt Disney's "The Jungle Book" that inspired me, although I didn't know it at the time. Singing along with King Louie the Ape as he swung through ancient ruins, covered by interwoven roots and branches of the enveloping jungle, entertained me as a child and still does so today. It turns out that this place actually exists. It's all still there in Angkor Wat, including the monkeys.
Angkor Wat is Cambodia's jewel; it is even depicted on their flag. There is less of a 'discovered in the jungle' feel to it these

days as four million visitors a year can confirm. But a visit to the world's largest religious site, all four hundred acres of it, was hugely rewarding for me.

It was built by the Khmer King Suryavarman in the early 12th. Century to worship the Hindu god Vishnu, but gradually became a Buddhist Temple by the end of the century. Angkor means City, and Wat is the Khmer word for Temple. As so often happens with Kingdoms, family arguments followed, neighbours invaded, the empire collapsed, and in this case the jungle swallowed it. Fast forward five hundred years to the 20th Century, and the world started to uncover it again. The Cambodian civil war and other interferences interrupted the recovery between 1970 and the late 80s. That makes it all the more remarkable that so much of it remains in fabulous condition. The bas-relief sandstone friezes show very little sign of wear. You can even see some of the paint or pigment applied in places. Sadly most of the statues have been decapitated and can doubtless be found in museums and private collections around the world. There's only the odd bullet hole and shell repair evident.

There are many Temples in the area but Angkor Wat itself is the best preserved. The centre piece has three rectangular galleries, each raised higher than the other. The highest level has five towers; four in each corner and the largest one in the middle. A mountain-like design. There is a moat and an outer wall.

The reliefs show religious events and beliefs, as well as wars and daily life.

Angkor Thom was built a little later by King Jayavarman VII, and encloses a large temple in the centre. The faces on the towers are either images of the King himself, or of his guardians. Scholars are divided on the answer, but I liked them anyway.

Ta Prohm always makes visitors smile, whether you are a fan of Lara Croft, Indiana Jones or "The Jungle Book". This late 12th. Century Buddhist Temple complex has been left largely as it was found, except for some steel frames added here and there to support roofs and walls. Some of the huge trees - one species is called silk-cotton and another is called strangler-fig - engulf the walls with colossal roots both destroying and supporting the stone structures. Their roots reminded me of Kaa the snake in "The Jungle Book".

I find that after a while you can become a little overwhelmed by the contents of museums, as well as ancient monuments and cultures. One experience can blend in to another, and a full appreciation becomes more difficult. Angkor Wat stimulated me to the limit for its history, culture, architecture and craftsmanship. The vibe of modern cities beckoned, and I moved on.

Kuala Lumpur, Malaysia surprised me. I stayed right in the centre and found it to be packed full of modern urban life. The city felt very successful. In fact, the whole of Malaysia felt successful. Prices were low but rising. Taxes were rising to allow the Government to balance the books after years of heavy investment. There is clearly some individual wealth, but many told me their salaries were not rising with prices. So, no surprises there then. Money has been spent well on education, housing and infrastructure. I left wanting to stay longer.

I think Kuala Lumpur may have had an eye on Singapore, my next stop. This city state was booming. Historically, it traded goods through the ports, between east and west, and now complemented that with a trade in information. Money basically. The central business district looked and felt like it should be in the world's top ten.

Jakarta, capital of Indonesia, does not feel like Kuala Lumpur or Singapore to me. I think fundamentally the traffic is the main problem. It is the world's largest city without a public transport network. Decades of debate, indecision and probably corruption are to blame. Congestion, air pollution, filth and inability to move efficiently, blight the city. Yet, its growth is admirable. Again, there is a very successful vibe here, but I think it could be better.
Nevertheless it is where my eldest son chose to settle a few years beforehand. He is an English teacher.

I arrived in Jakarta still without a clear idea of when my bike might arrive from India. It was beginning to look like the original arrival estimate was going to be missed with a large margin of error. After the customs delay in Delhi, it was then delayed crossing India by train, delayed again at the port in Nava Sheva waiting for a vessel, delayed again getting to Singapore, delayed again changing to a different vessel there, and delayed again leaving Singapore. Unfortunately I now had no choice, despite chasing my agent every other day, but to accept that one man with one oversized motorcycle on a one way route around the world, unlikely ever to return their way again, has no ability whatsoever to negotiate a better deal, or demand better service.

Yet again I was going to have to re-think my schedule. I remember commenting to a friend in this period that whereas I had previously thought that running a business involved making a great many decisions in any working day, I was now wondering if the process of riding around the world was even more complex. Certainly there were many factors affecting every decision. They were all inter-related. Every decision had a consequence. Problems emerged at every turn, and as before, I had to re-learn that every problem had to have a solution. On my journey almost every decision involved acquiring more knowledge before the decision could be made. This knowledge was rarely acquired from one source as I felt the need to solicit the opinion of others as well as evaluate the service required. The process of port procedures was also exacerbating. Every time my bike crossed water it had to be first fitted inside a wooden box, and strapped down. It was not possible for it to be transported directly inside the sea container, strapped down, but inside a wooden box, then inside the sea container. I was obliged to show that the wooden box had been FSC marked, and fumigated. I understood FSC - Forest Stewardship Council - but was further frustrated by the excessive use of TLAs - Three Letter Acronyms - in the shipping world. I had to learn LCL, CAF, THC, SAC, CBM, and MTS to name a few. Not to mention learning about why I had to pay for a Bill of Lading, Handling charges, Documentation charges, Delivery Order charges, Currency depreciation charges, Liner D.O. charges, Stuffing charges, and Destuffing charges.

I had hoped to have the bike immediately after arriving in Jakarta, and ride directly to my son, then around Java and eventually to Bali. However, the natural order of things got completely jumbled up. Part of the disappointment was because I couldn't wait to see my son, Oliver. He had married Fina a year earlier and shortly after announced that they were expecting a baby. Their news arrived in London in time for Sue to receive it, just a couple of weeks before she passed away. She was ecstatic to learn that she would become a grandmother.

They live in Bogor, south of Jakarta, where I was greeted with a bemused glare from my first granddaughter, Qaleesya. We all spent a glorious week together, but the conversation often turned to their grieving for Sue. I was also able, to some extent, to talk to them about Dalila. This was my first opportunity to do so. I continued to accept the view that I had met her too soon, without challenging them. They were right. My other son, Ben, harboured the same view. He had flown out from London to meet me in Dubai, and was clearly reluctant to talk about her. It was evident that I needed to bide my time. Time in fact was on my side as I still had about two thirds of my journey ahead of me.

― ― ―

However, it was Dalila time again. She flew out to Bali, as did I, whilst my illusive bike was still at sea. In fact I was there a couple of days before her to meet with some shipping agents to arrange my eventual onward passage to Australia. It wasn't easy to track down anyone who could help me. In fact, the prospect of me riding around Java in a circle and back to Jakarta was becoming a distinct possibility. Not the end of the world. Eventually I learnt that Bali has a 'Deus Ex Machina" outpost. This Australian business started with custom motorcycles but has evolved into a clothing brand. In fact their presence on Bali turned out to be largely a cafe / bar. I approached them to see if they shipped bikes to or from Bali to Australia. No reply. I found two other smaller custom motorcycle businesses on the island and asked the same question. Yes, they did, and each referred me to their shipping agent. Thanks to them, I settled on one man who seemed confident in the process.

I met Dalila at the airport with a now familiar routine and greeting. She did not have a question prepared for me this time. Our first day was spent on a beach and in the sea, where we repeated the "Jaws" overture and Frankie Valli song moment, several times. The next few days were spent being tourists, visiting temples, lakes, waterfalls, terraced rice fields, a batik workshop, a coffee plantation and some hilarious moments riding an elephant. We also bought each other engagement rings, and had prepared a few words to say. Dalila thought that a romantic evening boat trip around a bay would be the perfect occasion for our exchanges. We chatted to a Scottish couple who offered to take photos of our moment, and slipped off quietly to the bow together. The rings and vows were exchanged dutifully and romantically, before turning to discover that every one of the other fifty passengers had realised what we were doing, and were hanging on to the railings, leaning over them to get a better view. They applauded us warmly.

Our airport departure was as difficult as ever, involving tears, and ending in another reminder that I was still heading in the opposite direction, around the world. In fact I was only heading back to Jakarta, at last with a promise that my bike was almost there. A few more frustrating days of bureaucracy and payments followed before we could be re-united.

I headed south to Bogor again, this time on my bike. That was easier said than done. Jakarta's suburbs seem endless, especially in the heat of the 38°C. midday sun. I was making slow progress on the road, but the sweat was making rapid progress inside my leathers. I knew the bike was getting hot too as the temperature warning light was spending more time on than off. I had not seen this before. Pulling away from a set of lights, the bike exploded in front of me. Liquid shot in every direction, spraying cars to the left and right, as well over me. My visor was open so I took a sprinkling over my face, immediately recognising that it was radiator coolant, not oil or fuel. I pulled over as it hissed and spewed to a halt. This was not a good moment. I feared a fatal explosion had just broken my unbreakable Rocket.

Quickly grabbing my Water-to-go bottle, I rinsed my face clean. All was well with me. The front half of the bike was covered in its dirty brown coolant, but not much was left on the ground. I was sure that the radiator had burst open, but couldn't find a hole. Glancing down I spotted a small split in a short section of hose just below it. There was no other evidence of a fault, but I realised I was not going to make any further progress without help. A phone call to Triumph back in Jakarta was my sole plan in the event of a breakdown or puncture in Indonesia. Frankly, calling the nearest Triumph dealer in any country was my sole plan anyway. Although I had needed a small seal replacing in Istanbul, and a service in Dubai, I had nevertheless called in to introduce myself at a number of Triumph dealers on my journey so far. I thoroughly enjoyed meeting dedicated members of the Triumph family, engaging in a little mutual promotion, and putting a smile on some faces. In the back of my mind I always thought that, if I needed their help later on, then the prior introduction might help. It did. The breakdown trailer was immediately despatched and the manager attended to me immediately on arrival. Prior to fitting a replacement short section of hose, his diagnostic computer pinpointed the cause of the problem. A fuse had blown. It ran the coolant pump. Whilst they carried out further checks I stepped over the road to a cafe and was instantly attracted to the decor. Every wall, as well as the ceiling, was plastered in football memorabilia, mostly from the English Premier League. I met the owner who pointed out the scarves of some of the matches he had attended. They included many F.A. Cup Finals and Champions League Finals. This guy was a real fan. The cafe turned out to be a side-line to his main business running an on-line football commentary channel in Indonesia. Haris Pardede and I have remained friends, even though he supports Arsenal.

Four hours after the hose had blown, I was on my way again and offered warm thanks to the service team at Triumph. Night had fallen as I arrived in Bogor. The following morning allowed all the family to get some memorable photos of myself and Qaleesya on the tank of the bike. "Cool Grandpa" they called me as we recorded the moment with three generations sat on one very large bike, ridden all the way there from London.

I chose a diagonal route out of Bogor, but felt slightly lost for most of the afternoon, passing chickens and goats in the road, and paddy fields all around. The first sign for a hotel did not appear until late in the day, and amused me with a series of firsts. After agreeing to eat the one item on the menu that was available, it arrived in my room half an hour later in a take away box. The bathroom had a tap on the wall where a shower might have once been fitted, and the space for a basin looked as if it had been empty for even longer. I decided to leave early the following morning, but couldn't until I had cleaned off the extraordinary amount of guano that had been deposited on my bike overnight. I had parked it under a tree with a colony of small bats.

Java was a beautiful island to ride through. The countryside was lush, green and tropical. All the fields were full of animals and crops of every kind, and were busily tended. The traffic, though, came to a grinding halt approaching every town. Trucks and buses belched in my face as drivers tried to get through. For a greater part of my journey I ran parallel to a toll road running west to east, but it was too expensive for much of the local freight traffic to use. I felt slightly aggrieved to learn that motorbikes were not allowed on them, despite my engine being bigger than in almost every car.

I had been advised that I was highly likely to be stopped by the police, whose principal goal seemed to be to take a little bit of money from me for the staff biscuit tin. That didn't happen until my fourth day on the road in Java. I was prepared for them. First out of my pocket was my passport which prompted a puzzled look at my number plate. I quickly followed it by showing my

UK registration documents and Carnet. I took half a step backwards to check that all was progressing in the direction I had expected. Half a step forward again, with a huge smile on my face, I took the documents back from the officer and announced that all was OK. He had no idea what he was looking at anyway. I then asked them if they would like a photo of the bike. Six mobile phone cameras appeared without a second thought, as one by one they took a selfie of themselves with the Rocket. Someone else took some shots of all of them surrounding me: a photo that became one of my most cherished. Did it prove that putting a smile on their face was more important than money after all?

Deep in mountainous central Java lay the world's largest Buddha site - Borobudur - my next stop.
In the late 9th. Century the successful ruling dynasty of the region combined the indigenous cult of ancestor worship with the Buddhist concept of attaining Nirvana, employing Javanese Buddhist architecture, but this time on a grand scale. There are nine stacked platforms, six square and three circular, with a central dome on top. Two thousand six hundred and seventy two relief panels (I didn't count them), some in better condition than others, left me awe-struck and a little overwhelmed. There are also five hundred and four Buddha statues. As with Angkor Wat, most were headless, thanks to thieves, museums and private collectors around the world. What remains though was magnificent. It was huge, and felt masterful.
Severe water erosion, high temperatures, the jungle, earthquakes and volcanic ash deposits have done their best over the millennium to destroy the temple. Support from British then Dutch rulers, and later German and Unesco funding, have combined to preserve and sustain the site. Despite heavy rain when I visited, it still managed to enthral me.

Another couple of days riding got me on to Bali, arriving well after dusk again. The risk was not necessary to take as I arrived well within time to *rendez-vous* with my shipper. However, it allowed me an extra day to line up another photo. This one was set above a surfing beach. I commandeered a dutch tourist to snap away for me when a bikini-clad, slender young lady walked behind me carrying a surf board on her head. I turned to admire her, just as he took the shot. Another favourite in the bag.

Just along the shore from there was a Hindu Temple. I approached up a few steps and saw a large sign which offered visitors advice on how to behave. The first two bullet points had the usual counsel about covered shoulders and sombre dress, but the third recoiled me backwards. It stated that menstruating women were not allowed in to the temple. I was flabbergasted. I had not seen a notice like this before that moment. I took a minute to reflect but could not calm myself down, and left without venturing inside. To me this was misoginism at its worse. It must be a rule invented by men, I decided. Without the menstrual cycle the human world would come to an end. That would include no more men too. Just because a woman was menstruating should not preclude her from entering her temple to pray. I had observed in India, and to a lesser extent on Bali too, how dedicated Hindus are to their religion. I had learnt how vitally important it was for them to pray and make offerings every day, and that their temple was the focus for that activity. And yet they were excluded from doing so when menstruating.

Some time later I learnt that the Muslim faith has a similar view on menstruation, preferring to 'excuse' women from having to pray in a Mosque at this time.

I think I was probably at a tipping point anyway, but these discoveries pushed me over the edge. I was now able to come to a conclusion about my lifelong struggle with religion, and announce "I am not religious".

The earlier visit to Ireland, and subsequent thoughts I had about the so called apparition, enabled me to very nearly come to a conclusion about Christianity. My time spent in Turkey, the Middle East and Indonesia enabled me to come to some sort of a conclusion about the Muslim faith. Buddhism is not a religion but I gave it some thought whilst I was in Nepal. My time in India and now on Bali enabled me to come to a conclusion about

Hinduism too. For me personally, perhaps very personally, I have decided that none of them are credible. The basics are helpful for moral guidance, and usefully supplement the parental educational process, but it's the details which I cannot reconcile. It's the details which separate one religion from another, and it's these details which cause conflict, wars and death.

— — —

The usual round of export shipping routine followed. My bike was cleaned, crated and sent, would you believe, back to Jakarta, for onward shipment by sea to Brisbane, Australia. To avoid any further time wasted waiting for my bike to arrive somewhere, I checked three times with Wayne the shipper - twice verbally and once in writing - that my bike would only take thirty days, including all the port processing, to get from A to B.

Meanwhile, I planned to spend some time in New Zealand on a hired bike. After much consideration, I decided that riding a hired bike was better than not going there at all. Doing that would also save me a great deal of money shipping my bike in and out of New Zealand before it had to cross the Pacific Ocean. There were no Triumph Rockets available for hire, sadly, so I settled on another Triumph - a Tiger 800.

9. Time to reflect with some very good lemonade.

Over the years I had loved thumbing through the pages of the world's greatest travel magazines, and had noticed how remarkably consistently New Zealand topped the lists of reader's favourite destinations. Several of my closest friends had been, and all agreed it was their favourite too. This was to be my first visit.

Starting south of Auckland on the small Coromandel Peninsula took me all of the first day to ride. I simply had to stop after almost every turn to admire the view. Each was picture perfect, one after the other. A copse, a stream beside a little field, a seaside bay, the crest of a hill, the distant view, the manicured meadows, were all absolutely perfect. What a start! I loved the mix of familiar British place names with the Maori names. They made me smile. So too did the people. As friendly as I had always believed they would be. I was also particularly enjoying speaking English again to native English speakers.

On my first night I was pleased I had ordered a Cheeseburger and fries. I'd probably overdosed on them in recent years in London, thoroughly enjoying the plethora of new restaurants offering craft or gourmet burgers. So far on this trip I had avoided reverting to a burger, always wanting to choose a local option. In New Zealand the local option, or at least one of them, turned out to be burgers. It was truly delicious, carefully assembled with local Angus beef, as well as other fresh ingredients. Beer or wine had increasingly slipped away from being my drink of choice in Asia, but of course I was happy to reverse that phase too, enjoying some of New Zealand's finest as the first week unravelled.

I have an absolute rule not to drink alcohol and ride, recognising that I was a lucky man to have survived too many foolish moments when I was a teenager. So in the middle of a riding day

I would often choose to drink lemonade, but only if it was homemade.

Iran made lemonade quite well; India even better. Much of south east Asia made a pretty good job of it too. New Zealand's offering was bordering exceptional. By now I had decided that picking fresh lemons from trees nearby was most likely to make a better lemonade than transporting them from somewhere else. In fact, many years ago I decided that most fruits picked directly from a tree, perfectly ripened, and warmed by the sun that day, were the pinnacle of pleasure. Memories of eating figs from a tree in Greece, oranges from a tree in Spain, and apricots from a tree in France, have been impossible to forget. "Oh bliss! Oh rapture! Oh poop poop!" , as Toad said in Kenneth Grahame's book, 'Wind in the Willows'.

The second ingredient for making lemonade is sugar. I felt sure that in Asia it was sometimes made with raw sugar cane, clearly seen growing in fields on my route. I certainly saw it being shaved and pulped into something useable in open kitchens.

The third ingredient New Zealand had in abundance. Cool, fresh, spring water, and ice cubes made from the same. A sprig of fresh mint, not too much, topped off the drink nicely. I found the addition of a plastic disposable straw unnecessary.

Just for the record, the clear, over-sweetened, carbonated stuff that gets bottled by international drink companies is definitely not my choice.

It didn't take me long to reach the bottom of North Island. Wellington hosts the ferry service to South Island. Whilst waiting to board I was joined by five bikers on Harleys. They didn't immediately engage me in the usual conversations but kept themselves to themselves whilst fiddling with bits on their bikes. Eventually the slighter older of them came over. He warmed up when I got to the bit about riding around the world on the world's largest production motorcycle. He ran a motorcycle repair shop, and asked me more questions than I could answer about what was going on inside my engine. His girlfriend smiled at me, just as a lady in a particularly bright yellow hi-vis jacket came over. She was from the ferry company and announced to us all, one by one, "No *petches*". She repeated it until, one by one in return, we each nodded our head in acknowledgement. I had no idea what she was talking about. A New Zealand English accent could sometimes be a little difficult for me to understand. Nevertheless, I followed the others on board, strapped my bike into place beside theirs, and didn't see them again until disembarkation. It was only then, in the final stage before riding away, that I was able to translate "*petches*". She meant "patches". The instruction was to not display any sewn-on motorcycle club patches on our leathers. In the case of the Harley riders, this took the form of the leather vests they had now slipped over their jackets. They clearly displayed the fact that my new Harley friends were all ' Hells Angels'.

— — —

Entering South Island by water, in late afternoon sunshine, was a truly glorious experience. The ferry slipped effortlessly through a narrow channel, gliding left and right past rocky outcrops, forested hills, and mysterious inlets, before eventually revealing the small town of Picton. Following another hearty meal and good night's sleep, I rode for a while into empty countryside, stopping at a river overlook to reflect on the occasion. It was exactly 12 months ago, to the minute, that Sue had died.

I had lost my wife, the mother of our sons, my business partner, and my best friend. We also lost our business, just eleven days before she died, and in the same moment my income and at least half my pension plan.
I felt I needed to turn my life upside down to cope with the cavernous hole. To venture in to the world with an open heart and soul, to make myself vulnerable to its idiosyncrasies, and to ask the world to show me anything and everything it had to offer. It had certainly done that. I wanted to give the world something in return. To share the love that was within me, and still pouring out. To share some messages, and some of my passions.

I got on my bike in London, and today had reached South Island New Zealand. A long way from home, if I still had one, sitting on a bench staring at the view and wondering …. What the fuck just happened!

I had moments like this on a regular basis, but today I also thought about others who had grieved and struggled, perhaps more than me.

It had helped me enormously to focus on my journey, and the reasons for doing it. Not many people get presented with a chance to live an adventure, perhaps even a dream. On my journey I had implored people to take that chance, and not to dwell on it for too long. I had told many people that they would never regret it, but that they would certainly regret not trying.

I had met new people almost every day. I had met some fantastic people. Whether they wanted to hear or not, I told them that I was riding around the world to share two messages. The first message was to ride a motorcycle, as it could be so much fun. I was there to prove it to them. I could always see their eyes start to light up when they began to register what I was telling them. Then they started to grin; then their jaw dropped open. I had made a difference to their day, possibly their life. The second message was to ask them to please stop smoking. This message did not make them grin. I explained that Sue smoked, Sue got cancer, Sue died. Then they would tell me of a loved one who died. A close family member or just a friend; it mattered not. The fact was that they all knew someone who had died from smoking.

If the conversation permitted, or seemed relevant, I would tell them too about my passions for Chelsea Football Club, The Royal Geographical Society, Triumph Motorcycles and the Ted Simon Foundation.

Rethinking the reasons for my journey was always a useful process at the best of times. On this day, it seemed particularly poignant. Waking from my sub-conscious trance, I felt revived, even happy. I knew I was doing the right thing. I knew why I was doing it. I felt good about doing it.

New Zealand's roads were in excellent condition, and particularly welcome after months in Asia. Short sections of roadworks were very well managed with a plethora of people in yellow jackets waving me down well ahead of those working in the construction area. I felt safe. The greatest danger was my complacency which every now and then led to unfortunate encounters with wildlife. I lost count in the end but regretted every one of the rabbits, rodents and birds that crossed my path before I was able to take avoiding action. Sorry New Zealand. However, I particularly enjoyed riding over their 'One Lane Bridges'. I wasn't sure why but they amused me. Perfectly good two lane roads would become one lane roads when crossing ditches or rivers. Some had a wooden surface and others had a metal grid. Warning signs for motorcyclists told me to slow down and expect a rumble noise, but in fact I found that they decreased my stability. Eventually I learnt to cross them with confidence and a little more speed, but it took a while.

The west coast of South Island, from Greymouth to Haast, was green. I mean, really green. The greenness rose above me most of the way. Ancient woodlands, including ferns, hid the landscape from view by their density, abruptly ending right at the edge of the road. Through the tighter sections walls were covered with an untamed natural carpet of lush green vegetation. Heavy rain, on and off, added to the mystery with a ghostly mist, but frequent stops for photographs, when the sun pierced the day, helped me capture many moments of joy. Short detours to the Fox and Franz Joseph glaciers surprised me by their accessibility and proximity to the coast. It was all so beautiful.

Swinging inland I arrived at Queenstown realising that I was hopelessly underprepared for it. There are more mountains, lakes, activities, adventure sports and tourists there than I had imagined. My ride through it all was utterly inadequate to appreciate it, but there was a stop I just had to make. The Kawarau Gorge Suspension Bridge is the home of bungy jumping, where it all started in 1988. I was advised to leave my bike keys in reception, but otherwise headed to the edge in full leathers. Cameras captured me exclaiming "This is mad!", as I leapt off. The palpitations at that moment disappeared instantly as I floated, arms outstretched like a featherless eagle, hurtling towards the river below, before returning skywards in slow motion. More bliss, rapture, and poop poop.

After reaching the southernmost point at Bluff, I turned around and headed north to Invercargill. I could still hear Anthony Hopkins pronouncing the name of his character's home town in the film, "The World's Fastest Indian", as I stopped at E. Hays & Sons hardware store. The heavily modified 1920 world record breaking Indian Scout known as the Burt Munroe 'special' was exhibited there. There's also an amazing collection of other memorabilia including a 1969 BSA Rocket 3, the forerunner to my beast.

Over the next week I rode ever steadily northwards, appreciating the beauty and variety of both islands. The country used to be famed for having twenty head of sheep for every person. I learnt that this ratio was slipping, and that the dairy and cattle industry was larger now, attributable to substantial exports, mostly to China. Just by riding past it all I was able to observe what appeared to be a healthy agriculture industry. Everything was growing well; avocados, Manuka trees for honey, kiwi fruit and wine grapes amongst many others. The country's isolation had limited the need for pest control and widespread use of pesticides. I saw the spread of wild flowers as evidence of that. South Island had wild Lupins growing freely at the borders of many fields and streams, whilst North Island had wild Agapanthus. Unfortunately they are prolific in some places, and officially considered to be a weed. I thought their abundance was beautiful.

After some particularly interesting conversations in a Maori owned hotel, I reached the northern most tip at Cape Reinga. Taking a leisurely stroll to a small lighthouse and tourist signpost, I learnt that I was nearly ten thousand nautical miles from London. There was a family there for company. The children were excited to have arrived, no doubt at the end of a long journey in a car. The grandfather, who had probably seen it all many times before, came over to say hello to me. "Why was I travelling alone?", he asked. One of the usual questions. I blurted out my reply, watching his reaction change as I spoke. He had no doubt heard it all before as well, but we warmed to each other immediately. I enjoyed our conversation as we talked about shared life experiences. He expressed admiration for my positivity in the face of adversity, finishing with the proverb "If life gives you lemons, make lemonade".

I had heard this before, or something like it, and felt flattered that he had attributed it to me. Lemons suggest sourness or something not too pleasant. Certainly, a blow. Making lemonade is turning them into something positive and enjoyable.

As I strolled back up the coastal path, I made the mistake of considering the more literal interpretation of the proverb. What was wrong with lemons, I wondered? They are sour but I like them for that characteristic. They reminded me of drinking a long gin and tonic on early summer evenings, squeezed on to fresh fish, or added to any number of recipes. Lemonade was good too, especially the home-made kind as I had already discovered in New Zealand. He did not mean it to be taken literally of course.

I returned to the proverb many times over the following days, weeks and even months. He had in fact been quite accurate in his assessment of my positivity, in a way I had not previously acknowledged. I had not given myself enough credit. Leaving the UK after losing so much, traveling half way around the world, with an open heart, and overcoming all obstacles so far, can only be achieved by being positive, surely? Thank you sir, whoever you were, for making such a difference.

— — —

After three thousand miles I reached the end of my glorious ride, back in Auckland. By now I had decided that the country was as beautiful as everyone had told me. It probably contained, I concluded, everybody's top ten perfect natural views; they were all here. Mountains, hills, trees, fauna, beaches, lakes, rivers, glaciers, wild flower meadows, ancient forests and so on. But as always it was the people who made the difference. One lady's story surpassed all others. I stopped for breakfast in a small cafe on arrival in Auckland. One gentleman left, leaving just her and I. As I was dressed head to foot in black leather, with my helmet on the table, it was quite easy to start the usual conversation with me. We were about the same age. Within three minutes we were both talking about the loss of our spouses, and our eyes were watering. She had struggled with her loss, more than me, but seemed genuinely taken with my positivity and ambition to seek something else in the world. I gave her my visiting card, and left. A few hours later a long email arrived from her. "OMG Mark, you've changed my life. I'm going to do it. I'm going to go on a motorcycle adventure of my own." She and her late husband had owned their own farm. She had now sold it, but explained to me that it was her, not him, who held the responsibility for maintaining all the farm equipment. Whilst doing so she sometimes wondered not about looking after the tractors, but about looking after a motorbike. There was something of an adventurer in her, but she had never had an opportunity to explore it. It seemed that, quite by chance, I had now given her the motivation to get on two wheels, and explore. There was just one issue to resolve. She had never ridden a motorbike.

I referred her to the local Triumph dealer who I visited later that morning. We exchanged a few emails over the next month, but then she went quiet on me for a while. Eventually I received the news that I had been so hoping would follow. It contained a photo of her, an enormous smile, and her new motorcycle test certificate. She had passed!

She bought a bike, and announced her travels plans to me. The first tour was to be South Island New Zealand. A perfect choice. I couldn't be happier for her.

10. I exist.

Although I love cities, Auckland seemed busy and expensive after all that countryside. I dropped the Tiger back at the hire company, and headed for the airport. All was good with my forward plans, but I couldn't help thinking, again, that I was taking far too many flights for a journey around the world by road. The next two flights ahead of me, a journey totaling 34 hours, had a bonus in store. In fact, the very biggest one imaginable. Dalila. I went back to Lyon for Christmas.

I arrived with preparations in full swing for the fortnight ahead. We busied ourselves with some shopping, but mostly spent the days before the 25th with her friends, my new friends. I announced to them all, one by one, that "I exist". It seemed important for me to joke that I was not a figment of her imagination, and that I was a real person. Not just someone Dalila had invented as she shot off here and there to see me in various exotic places around the world. I met most of her large family too and was made to feel extremely welcome. Somewhat cowardly I decided not to hop over to England with her as it was still clear that my immediate family could not accept that I had met someone and fallen in love again so soon after Sue's passing. It was to be a decision that I could put off for another day, especially bearing in mind that I had left them all to ride around the world, and was still only half way to that goal.

We spent the new year period with more of her family and friends in the heart of Burgundy. The hospitality, food and wine were excellent, and whetted my appetite for the future. We did not need to be re-assured that committing our lives to each other needed confirmation, but somehow felt that every day, every hour even, and everything we did together, helped us feel more and more comfortable with our decision.

No sooner had I arrived than it was time to go. I had a *rendez-vous* scheduled with my Rocket for the first week in January 2018, in Brisbane, Australia.

11. Crazy little thing called love.

Truthfully, I had been thinking a great deal about love in the months leading up to the end of 2017, and continued to do the same once the new year had arrived. It made me cry, at times, and brought uncontrollable joy, at others. I remember learning years before that the Inuit people of the Canadian Arctic had about seventy different words for snow, one for each of the many different forms it takes throughout their year. I was wondering now why we only have one word for love. There are many different ways to describe it of course, but still only one word for it. Somebody told me that for them this little four letter word had a hundred different meanings. I love my family and close friends, although each one is loved differently. I love chocolates and good red wine, though each of them differently too. I love everyone I have met on my journey. Some of them more than others of course, but I feel love for them all nonetheless.
Perhaps I should try and give everyone and everything a score on a kind of love scale, I wondered.
I would give the ones I love the most nine out of ten. My closest friends and immediate family. If I wasn't sure about someone then I would have to give them an eight. I would give things like my favourite travel memories, the smell of fresh coffee in the morning, the sound of a V-8 engine, the feel of new clothes, a seven or a six, and so on. No one would get a zero. A one was the lowest I would go. That space would be reserved for people who had stolen from me over the years. I couldn't give them a zero as they must have some redeeming quality, somewhere in their soul. I would put pigeons at the bottom too. Or more precisely, pigeon shit. Too much of the foul stuff had landed on my head, my shoulders, my bike and my windows over the years, even down my chimney pot. How do they get their evil excrement to fly so accurately in my direction? However, I can't even give pigeons a zero. Their stupid walk makes me laugh so much. Thinking of zero led me to another conclusion. If the

opposite of love is hate, and no-one gets a zero, then I had to eliminate the word hate from my vocabulary. Did I really not hate anyone or anything any more? Possibly. I vowed to try and not use the word hate in conversation. It would be an interesting test.
There can be only one person who gets a ten out of ten.

In Australia I was to meet several people and talk to them about love. I think I must have been ready to do so. The conversations were never expected or planned. They just happened, when the moment was right. To an extent I was trying to articulate a series of thoughts that had been happening inside my helmet for many months. Trying to explain to myself how I was feeling about Sue, and the many memories that kept flashing in front of me. I was also trying to understand why I had found it so easy to fall in love with Dalila. It had been such a surprise to me. The conversations all happened with people younger than me, some considerably so. The age difference seemed to give my thoughts a kind of advisory feel. Some were with men, but most were with women. They went something along these lines:

" Open up your heart and soul wider than you ever thought possible. You might need to make some physical changes to help this happen. Take a different route to work, order a different drink at a bar, or buy some new clothes. Try doing things to make yourself feel differently about yourself. You don't need to do something as dramatic as I did: get on a motorbike, leave everyone you have ever loved behind, and ride around the world. As you make these physical changes, try to think differently too. Overcome some of your inhibitions. Find the courage to walk up to complete strangers and start a conversation. Peel back the layers of prejudice you have built up over the years. You've got them, you know you have. I left London with both of these I am sure. I think they have all gone now, or at least very nearly."
I loved talking to people, to strangers, about anything. I loved listening to them.
The thing about solo travel is that you have to do this.

"If you are solo, alone, then there is no difference between being a traveller or being at home. Venture out of yourself." I demanded.

I would tell them about my love scale, from one to ten, and explain to them why I wanted to stop using the word hate.

" Let love pour out of you. It will find a home one day. After opening up your heart, after deciding to love everybody and everything, you will start to feel elevated. You will start to feel your smile widen. Walk around with a kind of Mona Lisa enigmatic smile. Quite possibly when you are least expecting it, Cupid will shoot his arrow. Watch out!"

" When you think you have found the right person to share your life forever, until death parts you, you must commit whole heartedly. Don't just try and see how it goes for a while. Don't move in together for a trial period. Jump in. If you are not sure if that might work, then don't bother. If you are certain, if you can't offer yourself any other explanation than 'it feels right', then it probably is. It won't be perfect, it never is. The challenge to keep it going is always stimulating. The secret to making it work, forever, is compromise."

A couple of these conversations were interrupted as they explained that they had tried all of this before, but it hadn't worked for them.

" It has taken me a very long time to understand that this one word, compromise, is the key to success. We humans have far more in common with each other than we have to separate us. We are genetically all much the same. Some differences in upbringing, experiences, culture, as well as race and creed give us some healthy and stimulating differences. You won't always agree on everything. You won't always feel you want the same things in life. You might even think that you are 'drifting apart'. The simple solution to all of these issues is to compromise. You have to talk until you reach some kind of agreement. Both of you. Just a little should be enough to repair things. I am the first to admit that reaching a compromise is far easier to say than achieve. One of you may well feel you are being asked to compromise far more than the other. Next time, the other person might be feeling that more. If a marriage feels like it might be breaking down, repair it. Don't throw it away. The reward for compromise is a life of ever increasing joy. A warm, cosy, enveloping, all-embracing, gooey kind of love.

A love so profound you won't be able to describe it. My journey around the world, half of it to this point, has taught me so much about it, and especially its people. However, there is something I knew a while ago, but have re-discovered. It is simply that the greatest thing in life to learn is to love, and, be loved in return."

There are some pertinent lyrics by Freddy Mercury in Queen's 1980 song "Crazy little thing called love":
I gotta be cool, relax, get hip
And get on my track's
Take a back seat, hitch-hike
And take a long ride on my motorbike
Until I'm ready
Crazy little thing called love

12. The tyranny of distance.

My first day in Australia left me gasping to contain my frustration, and pleading for better news. Despite asking for updates on the sea passage of my bike from Indonesia to Australia, and receiving little but waffle in return, I nevertheless still expected to be reunited on time as agreed. The Australian end of the Bali team had just told me it was not expected to arrive for a further three and a half weeks. The thirty day promise from the agent in Bali proved to be worthless. I had assumed the polite Balinese gentleman of good character to be honest, but reluctantly concluded that he acted with a level of incompetence that I had so often experienced throughout Indonesia. He didn't think to tell me about a delay due to a customs inspection leaving Surabaya on Java, and didn't think to tell me that, as a consequence, it had missed the connecting vessel in Jakarta. He later said that Christmas schedules are different to the normal schedules, which he also failed to explain to me in advance. I would have at least expected that to be so, but apparently he didn't think to tell me. It had also transpired by this time that he failed to tell me that the company name on his business card, as well as on the invoice he presented to me for his services, was not in fact the name on his bank account. My direct bank transfer had arrived at his bank promptly, but they refused to allocate funds to him because the account name I used did not match their records. It took several weeks to unravel that little issue. At least I assume it got unravelled. He never confirmed it did; he just stopped chasing me.

After the elation I felt following such a glorious Christmas and New Year period with Dalila and her family, the crash to earth when I realised I had rushed to the other side of the world just to start another thumb twiddling period, was colossal. Moping around Brisbane for a few days, dazed and sour faced, my mood spiralled downwards. Unusually, I couldn't shake myself from it. Getting over jet-lag couldn't have helped either. For the first time on the journey I gave some serious thought about how to wrap it all up and go home. After all, I had left the UK asking the world to deliver me a new life, and it had done that.

The jet-lag eventually lifted, and so too did the cloud hanging over me. Of course I couldn't give up. I had to keep going, not just for my self-esteem, but for everyone else who was following, supporting and encouraging me every step of the way. I busied myself with formalities for the bike. I tracked down and found where I needed to go for an OVP - Overseas Vehicle Permit. This gave me temporary permission to ride my UK registered bike in Australia. I also needed to find where I could buy CTP - Compulsory Third Party Insurance. In a hidden office via a couple of telephone calls, it transpired, as all online systems failed to accept my license plate details. I also needed to offer my Carnet de Passage en Douane again, and to allow the bike to be inspected as part of Australia's quarantine regulations. Of particular concern were soil and seeds inadvertently carried in. Of course I was happy to oblige and had arranged for my Bali shipper to have the bike thoroughly cleaned before departure. I now had my fingers crossed.

The summer days rolled by. I enjoyed frequent visits to the Botanic Gardens as well as riverside walks. The Museum of Modern Art lured me in, several times, and other museums, shopping centres and cinemas did their best to keep me sane. I also visited the Triumph dealer, to say hi, and this time also to the BMW and Harley stores. I bought a new helmet as my old one had finally worn out. The visor mechanisms no longer worked well, and frankly the aroma inside was too much to bear, despite several vigorous washes.

Still bike-less, I took the train down to stay a couple of days with some very good friends in Byron Bay. They were great hosts, and distracted me from thinking about shipping companies for a while. It was a beautiful little town.

I also paid a visit to an old school friend who had been in Brisbane for many years. He had travelled by land across Asia in the 80s, and had followed me with such enthusiasm whilst I was there. I met his wife and daughters, and we chatted impulsively about life, schooldays and Chelsea Football Club.

Back in Brisbane, just around the corner from my hotel, was a travel shop offering short visits to almost anywhere in Australia, and a little beyond. I should have called in to talk to them earlier. A trip up to Cairns, and an opportunity to dive on the Great Barrier Reef, would certainly entertain me for a while. So off I went.

The taxi driver who took me from Cairns airport in to the centre of town was more interesting than most. As we both shared a passion for motorcycles I arranged to meet him later for a drink. He rode up on his exceptionally loud, heavily customised, 20 year old Harley. Being a Queenslander he had added crocodile skin to the bodywork, and changed the side stand for one with a chrome crocodile. I particularly liked that. The beers went down well and he started to open up to me. It transpired that this tough skinned lifelong biker had a soft centre. He rescued dogs for a local protection society, and supported an orphan elephant centre in Kenya, which I happened to know something about.
I booked him for my eventual return ride to the airport, and rounded up the fare to a higher than usual figure. A short while later I received an email from him to tell me he had given my gratuity to the Sheldrick Wildlife Trust in Kenya, making me part of his elephant fraternity.

I boarded the 'Ocean Quest' and was allocated a cabin with Irishman Ciaran. Not only did one of the usual conversations follow within minutes, but in the intimate world of our tiny cabin, it was able to expand in to quite a different place. We talked frantically and honestly for hours. I was still trying to conceptualise and clarify my new views on love, and did my best to justify them to him. He concurred, mostly, but had recently ended a long term relationship by mutual consent. He tried to persuade me they had made the right decision, but I could see he was not completely convinced. He had been living in Lyon of all places.

REBIRTH

I kept pinching myself trying to remember where I was. The Great Barrier Reef is a particularly special place; a precious and fragile space. One that the world had recognised as beautiful for a very long time, but now saw its declining health as a barometer for climate change. On my road trip around the world I had not imagined being ten metres under the surface of it at any point. But there I was, diving five times on two particular reefs over a three day period. I saw quite a few species I had not seen before. Barramundi Cod, Potato Cod, Mimic Surgeonfish, Spotted Boxfish, Mushroom Leather Coral, and Giant Clams. I even managed to get my photograph taken swimming with some Green Turtles.

--- ---

Sixty two days after I deposited my Rocket at the shipper in Bali, we were finally re-united in a warehouse in Brisbane. I needed to borrow a sledgehammer to unbox it this time, as a considerable number of wood frame sections had been hammered together with long nails, in contrast to the usual plywood panels. In Mumbai I was asked how I was going to ride away with my wooden crate. I tried to explain it was not mine, but belonged to the shipping company. They demanded a disposal payment from me, which in the end I managed not to pay. In Jakarta, the local team seemed very keen to acquire some useful wooden panels. The Brisbane team asked similar questions of me. This time I couldn't fain a misunderstanding, and my pile of largely broken wood was not much use to anybody. I offered them a disposal fee / beer money which was gratefully accepted. Just before leaving them I learnt that all they were going to do was to hurl the broken bits in to the skip that was within view just outside the warehouse door.

The front tyre had deflated in transit which left me with an anxious and wobbly first ride in Australia to the nearest fuel station. The short ride back to my city centre hotel was long enough for me to confirm that all was well with the bike, the sat nav too, and that I was well and truly ready for the journey ahead.

I set off the next morning with a huge smile on my face, so pleased to be back on the road again. I recalled a joke. 'Motorcyclists are crazy. First we start with a hot engine, then we fill up a fuel tank just above it, then we stick the whole lot between our legs.' If I was crazy, then it felt great. There were to be good roads ahead, English spoken at every stop, road signs I could read and understand, as well as a general familiarity that was not available to me in India and Indonesia. Confidence rose with every twist of the throttle. This was to be a very different adventure.

Friends had asked me why I wanted to head west from Melbourne. Kangaroos would leap out in front of me, red bulldust would find its way into everything, even my toothbrush, I would run out of fuel, I would run out of water, and I would run out of paved road. I had all of that in the back of my mind, and respected the advice. In fact I think I was hoping something might go wrong, but only slightly.

In his 1966 book, *The Tyranny of Distance*, Geoffrey Blainey explained how Australia's destiny had been shaped by its remoteness from Britain and Europe. The book's name was now liberally applied to describe the vast distances between almost anywhere in this colossal landmass.

Heading 'out west' from Brisbane the suburban sprawl and satellite towns petered out quite rapidly. Farming and other land management activities congregated around road intersections, and a rail track ran alongside the road for a while. It too petered out.

The long-legged, stocky and well-fleeced Merino sheep are the breed of choice here. After their introduction in the second half of the 19th century, the wool industry flourished. However, lower wool prices, a sheep shearer's strike, and a drought in the 1890s brought much hardship with it. These events inspired Banjo Paterson to write "Waltzing Matilda" in 1895. Its lyrics are sad, and end in death, but that has not stopped it becoming Australia's unofficial national anthem.

"Once a jolly swagman camped by a billabong

REBIRTH

Under the shade of a coolibah tree,
And he sang as he watched and waited 'til his billy boiled,
you'll come a-Waltzing Matilda, with me."

Waltzing Matilda, Waltzing Matilda
You'll come a-Waltzing Matilda, with me."

Banjo Paterson's life is celebrated in Winton, Queensland. A little further on I stopped at a 'Roadhouse' for fuel and water. In fact I decided after the advice given to me at the outset I should stop whenever one appeared, whether I was low on fuel or not. Every now and then the 'next' stop might be out of fuel. This roadhouse was particularly simple, small and run down. I sat with the ageing proprietress for a drink and snack. She shuffled across from the counter and sat in a threadbare armchair beside me. I commented on the sign entering her village which said the population was eleven people. I talked about my stop in Winton as she sorrowfully explained to me that the figure had now dropped to eight. She recalled the harsh life of the old man who had lived down the track opposite her roadhouse. He had known Banjo Paterson in his youth. Her husband, marginally less infirm than her, was busy fixing a plumbing issue in the roof-space. Life had become harsh for them, but of course she didn't complain. There was no point in whinging like a Pom out there. Nobody was there to listen.

Larger stations are dominated by beef cattle; Brangus and Charbray cross breeds, but the largest of all have mixed use. Probably wise to have some versatility, as the very largest of them run to over one million acres each.

I learnt a great deal when I visited the Australian Stockman's Hall of Fame exhibition in Longreach, Queensland. It contained a fascinating history of the development of the Outback. Just when I thought I was in the middle of nowhere, I learnt that my Queen had opened the building in 1988, principally to support the Royal Flying Doctor Service.

I just couldn't ride through Longreach without staying another night and visiting the second surprising museum it had to offer. There's an airstrip, and the Qantas Founders Museum. The airline started nearby, well quite near there anyway - it had an imprecise start - offering a flying postal service, marginally beating the rail service on speed and price. The history was also fascinating, as too were some of the earliest planes on display, but a tour of an early Boeing 747 was the highlight. I also learnt that Qantas is an abbreviation of Queensland and Northern Territory Aerial Services.

In this part of Australia, men are men, so I was told. Stockmen and miners are amongst the toughest. As if to emphasise this to me, I came across Crocodile Dundee's Walkabout Creek Hotel in Mckinlay, Queensland. There it was, complete with the bush vehicle used in the film.

Kangaroos line the roads in the dry season to lick early morning moisture from the bitumen. The unfortunate consequence, when startled by traffic, is that they leap in any direction and frequently in to oncoming vehicles. Local cars, utes and trucks all have kangaroo bars fitted, but motorcyclists are given stern warnings. I could easily be knocked off in the blink of an eye, or take avoiding action and end up in a slide. Some sections are so heavily littered with carcasses that it can look like a kind of kangaroo carnage at times. Emus, and wandering cattle pose a similar danger, but all make a welcome feast for the birds. Buzzards take the first pickings, then Crows, Thornbills and Spinifex pigeons follow. Further along, dead possums, wombats, boar and the odd koala added to my fascination for road-kill. I think it was the smell I liked, bizarrely. It was putrid, but I couldn't help looking for the carcass as I rode past.

The famous Australian Road Trains pull three articulated trailers, and can be up to fifty-three metres long. They seem to carry anything and everything needed for life in the Outback, as well as sheep and cattle to abattoirs. They weren't the unstoppable menace that I had been warned about. Overtaking was easy enough as the roads had so little traffic on them. The roads themselves were also particularly straight and mostly flat for as far as the eye could see. Early one morning I stopped to take a photograph of a kangaroo warning sign, as tourists do, and was amazed to spot the fact that my sat nav showed the next junction to be 389 miles ahead, down the Barkly Highway. The scale was difficult for a Brit from a small island to understand. But I loved it. There was a peacefulness which seemed to slip inside my leathers and reach my soul.

After riding west for a week I reached Threeways, in Northern Territory. It was just a road junction really but significant because it intersects with the Stuart Highway running north / south through the middle of the country. I headed south, and on towards my goal; The Red Centre.
This semi-official title spans four states. It is an ancient landscape whose oxidised red soil has worn fine, but supports diverse fauna. Amongst its native animals is the Quoll. It is a cute-looking carnivorous marsupial, but very much on the endangered list. I met a lady, Vicky, who was on her way to work as a volunteer in a Quoll conservation centre. We only met briefly in a Roadhouse to the north, but re-connected by chance down the road. I had stopped beside a sign which stated I was now in the geographical centre of Australia. Far too interesting for a Fellow of the Royal Geographical Society to ride past without wanting to know more. Stuart, the explorer, after whom the highway was named, calculated with a sextant that this spot was half way between the north and south coast, and almost halfway between the west and east coast. The spot most remote from any part of the coast, and the theoretical centre of gravity are nearby, but not quite where I was standing. However, a car travelled past, braked sharply, u-turned, and pulled up beside me. It was Vicky again. She opened up her car, lifted out her Esky - Australian brand of portable coolers - with fresh chilled milk inside, a packet of cereals, a bowl, spoon, and tablecloth, and then placed them all out on a shaded table beside me. We continued our conversation, starting with one of the usual questions; "Why was I travelling alone?" Yet again, although I should have seen this coming, we ended up shedding a few tears together. She had lost her lifelong partner too, and described his

death, just before retirement, as "very inconvenient of him". The Quoll conservation work was a helpful new focus for her.

I thought about the "very inconvenient of him" conversation many times after that. I think it was certainly another milestone in my grieving process. I knew I was not the only widower in the world, of course. I knew I did not want or demand sympathy from anybody. But I think I was still surprised when I met anyone in the same position. Hence the emotion, and the tears. I vowed after that not to reveal the same emotion again under the same circumstances. I stopped short of thinking that every solo traveller, of a similar age, was on their own because of a death. I had several friends back home who were there by choice.

Visiting Uluru was one of my goals when I set out from London, but it wasn't until I got there that I realised the enormity of the achievement. Not only is it in the middle of the middle, difficult enough to get to by any means, but even trickier on a motorbike, and trickier still on a Triumph Rocket. There was an enormous sense of pride within me when I arrived for the evening sunset photo opportunity that I had dreamed about for so long. The red rock turned a quite mystical shade, earthy inevitably, but also with a historical glow. It had been doing the same thing, night after night, for about 600 million years. That's a long time.
I snapped away for about half an hour, using a tripod and ten second delay, and eventually managed to capture the moment. I stood beside the bike with my arms folded, and legs apart. I felt I was half way around my world, and clearly displayed my pride.

Uluru had been better known as Ayres Rock, named after a British Chief Secretary of South Australia. It is also an important feature of the creation according to the local Anangu aborigines. Ownership was returned to them in 1985 but most tourists continued to feel that they must climb this culturally sacred site. The practice has now been banned. There are other red sandstone outcrops in the region, but Uluru is significantly taller than the others, reaching a height greater than that of the Eiffel Tour in Paris, a fact that surprised me.

In an engaging conversation with an Anangu Aborigine named Leroy, I learnt how to source and select fruits such as wild fig and bush plum, as well as bake with wattleseed. I also learnt how to source water from small pools at the base of trees with roots in cracks in the rock, as signposted by birds circling above. Handy tip.

The activities of other aborigines amused me. There seemed to be a widespread practice of dressing termite mounds. Some were covered with an old shirt, but others were more elaborately adorned with an old broom stick for arms, carefully inserted across the upper part of the mound. A shirt, jacket, wrap around skirt, hat and painted face added to their creativity. Sadly I learnt that alcohol was often the accelerant to these activities. I also saw a spectacular arrangement of old tyres dangling from a dead tree.

Waiting beside me at Uluru on the first evening were a couple from Switzerland. Stephen and Alexandra were good company, and full of the joys of adventure travel. They were on a world tour, in stages, using different means of transport, but not two wheels. They had a camper-van when I met them. In fact Stephen had grown up in Australia and regaled me with insights about life in the bush.
By now my roadhouse engagements were reaching a climax. It seemed, in the Outback, that conversations with extraordinary people, was in fact quite normal. There were so few people there, and almost nowhere to stop except at roadhouses, that new encounters were easy. At another stop I met a small group who were on an overland trip by bus from London to Sydney. They had started in a different vehicle, with different groups leaving and joining at various stages. After the Asia section there were about a dozen remaining. A mini bus was hired for the last leg to Sydney, leaving a disparate and slightly eclectic bunch to complete the journey. There were two Chelsea Football Club supporters amongst them, one with a tattooed forearm to make it easy for me to recognise his allegiance. However, it was Michele, a Canadian, who sat with me to occupy the last empty seat available. We talked enthusiastically about our journeys, and

managed to meet up again, quite by chance, at another roadhouse further south. I was standing beside a television screen showing an iceskating tournament, trying to convince myself that if I watched it for long enough, I might cool down. It was over 40°C. outside. She decided not to have the same thought as her troop would be camping out tonight in the next town, and was already mentally preparing for another warm night under canvas. I headed for the same town and checked in to an air-conditioned cabin.

Coober Pedy was an extraordinary place, even by Outback standards. It was the largest opal mining town in the world. As I approached, after a hundred miles or so of the flattest landscape imaginable, I started to see little white piles of soil. These were the spoil tips from the mines, themselves little more than a hole in the ground. Signs warn you of unmarked holes, and advise you not to walk backwards. I felt a childish disappointment as that was exactly what I was planning to do here - walk backwards without looking behind me.

Michele was good company that evening as we shuffled around town talking to some locals, as well as staring at the bizarre shapes made from old metal objects like a car, plane and even what we took to be a spaceship. The kangaroo orphanage also attracted our attention, as did the several underground hotels. Apparently many of the inhabitants were people who did not really fit in anywhere else. The town certainly had that atmosphere about it. Later on I also met a newly arrived young lady from Maryland, USA, who had just left home to travel Australia and ended up in Coober Pedy. I admired her self confidence and bravery, and wished her well. She couldn't have been much older than sixteen.

People, friends even, had wondered why I wanted to ride through the Outback. Apart from warning me about spiders and snakes, they also told it was empty. I left feeling that nothing was further than the truth. So called 'Grey Nomads' - older people with grey hair - spend a great deal of time in the Outback, camping or caravaning, and just living their quiet life in the warmth. One day, that might appeal to me.

REBIRTH

On the southern edge of the Outback I rode through South Australia's vast wineries. Each one felt like grape farming on a massive scale, far surpassing the size of anything I had seen in Europe. Villages started to appear again, then larger towns and the odd commercial building. I was heading back towards civilisation, and was not necessarily looking forward to it.

The ocean finally appeared before me again, at Port Wakefield, South Australia, and swung me further south, then east.

13. Friends, old and new.

I had done my best to keep up with the succinct views offered to me by Derek, the 'good traveller' I had met in Istanbul. We saw eye to eye on many issues so I had been looking forward to catching up again with him some day. That day had arrived, as I had accepted an invitation to stay with him in Ballarat, Victoria.
This former gold mining town had invested well in its future, boasting several world class schools and universities now. It still felt wealthy to me, and had maintained its historical centre sympathetically. The Botanical Gardens proudly displayed statues of former Prime Ministers of Australia, in amongst its tree collection. Derek's period home felt like a private art collection and museum in every room. It was crammed full of the best examples of local craftmanship collected from his travels around the world. A unique collection from a uniquely different traveller.

Riding in the state of Victoria was rewarding. Winding roads filtering through beautiful landscapes just can't be beaten. Neither, I thought, could the famous Great Ocean Road. Well it was certainly beautiful, but too full of roadworks and slow moving tourists to enjoy much of a ride. Notoriously, it had been built by returning soldiers from the First World War; the so called 'diggers' had become expert at digging trenches. About half way along were the Twelve Apostles. These magnificent limestone stacks line the coast, just out to sea, and are clearly visible from a number of view points. You have to stand and stare at them for a while to appreciate their size against the ocean waves. Disappointingly the twelve apostles are now just eight and a half apostles, but that only seemed to matter to me, no-one else.

Forever the publicity seeker for my messages to the world, I was thrilled every time a publisher had covered me. To date that had included various UK based motorcycle magazines, as well as Triumph's online magazine called 'For The Ride'. I was particularly thrilled to have been contacted by Leigh Wilkins who was just starting a new online only magazine called 'Traverse.' Leigh featured my Iran passage, and asked me to get in touch if my journey took me anywhere near his home. I did. It's in Melbourne. We spent a few days energetically talking bikes, travel and the Australian bush. I received a further invitation from him to ride out with his motorcycle club the following weekend. About two dozen of us rode deep in to central Victoria and stayed in a place called 'Rusty Springs'. It is on the site of a former farmstead where the outlaw Ned Kelly grew up. There was a gloriously diverse bunch of people there, who made me feel very welcome. Every conversation served to remind me of the pleasure of solo travel.

Back in Melbourne I met up with another new friend, Phil. We had met in a bar in Kathmandu, Nepal, where again I had accepted an invitation to stay with him once in Melbourne. We spent an emotional evening largely talking about life's difficulties and how to deal with them. In Uruguay, where he had lived for a few years, he was known as Felipe. In Melbourne he was back to Phil again, and very content with his life.

'Tassy' beckoned next. Tasmania. The island state off the bottom of Australia. It was a healthy, green island, boasting the cleanest air in the world as it produced its power hydroelectrically, not by burning fossil fuels. It also claimed the cleanest natural spring water too. I was taken by the look of the countryside, but the dated architecture left me feeling it had been left behind, a little.
Back home I had done some business over the years with an Aussie who had called his company after a steam train which had featured in his childhood. The Huon river ran down from the mountainous hinterland across his family's property, carrying timber on a steam train called the Belle. Hence his company was called Huon Belle. I could find no trace of the rail line or train, but quite by chance spotted a black and white photograph of it in the lobby of a hotel, crossing a large wooden viaduct over the valley.

Hobart, the capital, had an amusing installation in the Museum of New and Old Art. I was advised to go and see a row of plaster cast vaginas. It is called *Cxxxx and other conversations*, by Greg Taylor. I decided I could live without seeing it.

Heading back to the mainland, on a ferry packed with 'Grey Nomads' returning to the Outback after exchanging the extreme summer heat there for a cooler couple of months on the island, I came up with a neat little summary of my Tassy experience. I decided it was "like the British Isles used to be, but with gum trees".

Most of my journey up to Sydney went along the coast, but swung around the west of the city as I headed to a northern suburb to stay with friends, **Brett and Jane**. Jane has an interesting company, Signatur handknits, offering unique knitwear designs. She is also a successful author and educator.
The first of many highlights was to be a ride out with **Brett**, and some friends, **Nick and Craig**. Just for the day, it at least gave me a further insight in to the camaraderie that dominates the Australian biking community. In fact I spent half a day at work with **Brett**. We had known each other through our work in the film and television industries, spending at least a couple of decades each supplying the hardware required for production. The company that Sue and I had run for so many years was the appointed UK distributor for a number of Australian made products, amongst many more from around the world. No longer of course. He was now head of Arri in Australia, a world-leading camera and lighting company, and asked me to help with re-boxing some demonstration equipment after a series of exhibitions. I was happy to help and enjoyed being back in the industry if only for a few hours. We also caught up with another friend from the industry, Andrew. Importantly this day gave me an opportunity to reflect on the past, as well as my future. I thoroughly enjoyed being in the equipment environment again. I always loved the creative process of film production - my father had been a cinematographer before becoming a businessman - as well as having a fascination for the equipment used to achieve results. Cameras, lighting and related products had always

evolved over time, but exponentially so over recent years. I was handling some of the very best LED lighting systems that the industry now had to offer, albeit to just re-pack components with serial numbers into their original boxes. It led me to put some thought in to trying to return to the supply side of the film industry once I had finished my journey. I reflected on the fact that every other member of our company had been offered work after its collapse, but no-one had contacted me. It was probably difficult to employ someone who had been a business owner and something of an entrepreneur all their lives, after a business collapse. I also took that to mean that the industry had finished with me. It had made the decision for me, and that I had reached the end. That conclusion at least was helpful to me. I could now start to think about earning my living elsewhere. It was not to be selling this hardware any more.

I delivered my Rocket X to Sydney's main Triumph dealer. They were to service it and fit fresh tyres, before handing it over to my shipping agent. This time it was to be packed in to the largest Harley crate, which had a metal base and frame, together with cardboard side panels. A change from the usual wooden affair.
Also, by way of a change, it was to fly for the first time. The cost was competitive compared to sea freight, and saved me waiting while it traveled up to sixty days across the Pacific Ocean. I was heading for Santiago in Chile to start an altogether different adventure in South America.

In the meantime, after thanking my friends for their hospitality and moving to a small apartment in the centre, I enjoyed city life in Sydney for a few more days. The harbour, bridge, Opera House and other landmarks are all visible from the water's edge, and served to remind me that the city thoroughly deserves its status as one of the greatest in the world.
I met up with another old friend who had also worked in the television industry, Den. He had enjoyed a varied and successful career in London and was now putting all that experience together to offer business coaching to others in the creative industries. Sydney had become the perfect place for him to host his global organisation.

Quite by chance Sydney was building up to a big celebration whilst I was there. A parade wrapped around the area where I was staying so I couldn't miss it. It was Mardi Gras - the celebration of lesbian, gay, bisexual, transgender, queer and intersex life. It turned out to be great fun. A hugely excited crowd watched floats, parades, dancers, musicians and many other exotic, and erotic, entertainers. This community had a tough time in the past but with Australia's decision to permit same sex marriage by law the year before, they now had a great deal to shout about. The Prime Minister and other politicians were there, as was Cher, Dannii Minogue, and floats sponsored by many well known companies including Qantas. I wondered what the founders in Longreach, Queensland, might have thought of Mardi Gras. I was given, and cherished, a rainbow coloured wrist band by a policeman, parading with colleagues wearing just budgie smugglers and covered in sun tan oil.

Leaving the continent at Sydney airport led to another extraordinary encounter, this time over an identical looking MacBook Pro. Geraldine and I passed them through airport security at the same time, and decided one of us had better check that we had picked up the right one on the far side of the x-ray machine. All was OK, but, recognising my accent, she asked me where I was from. The Fulham and Chelsea border, I explained. She had spent her childhood on a road I knew well nearer the centre of Fulham. We continued to chat as we headed towards the gates together. It was one of those "why are you travelling alone" conversations, but at hyper-drive, as she was running a little late for her flight. She and her husband had discovered a special aboriginal water source in Queensland, and bottled it. They also ran a healing centre in France, and her daughter had become a successful Hollywood film director. Gerry was taken with my story too, but our whirlwind conversation was over in a matter of minutes. It ended with emotion showing in our eyes.

I grabbed a coffee and croissant, sat down, and stared at an illuminated sign over my shoulder. It read: ' I do believe it's time for another adventure'. A message just for me, I thought, as I boarded the flight to Chile.

14. Gormless Llamas.

There are only two ways to solve every little problem that arises when travelling solo. The first way is to solve it yourself, and the second is to benefit from the kindness of others.

When my bike was crated in Sydney the front tyre was deflated to fit in to the narrower slot that a Harley Davison tyre would fit in to. I had not been told about this, but it would not have made a difference anyway as the airport warehouse in Santiago where I collected it did not have a tyre inflator to hand. Of course it didn't, it was an airport warehouse. I didn't speak Spanish so I was on my own. In fact, things had been going well up to that point. I had been advised that there was no need to use a shipping agent in Santiago as the temporary import procedure for a bike was simple. I followed precise instructions given with ease, and was shown every courtesy at the airport and customs offices. It all took less than two hours. Foolishly, I had completely forgotten that in Dubai I had been given a small aerosol can of compressed air, now buried and forgotten about until I unpacked at the very end of my journey. I set off out of the airport complex and headed down a busy motorway, following directions to the first fuel station. I crawled and wobbled along in second gear, terrified that at any moment the tyre might peel off the wheel. I had to do the same in Brisbane, but this ride was much longer and much busier. **A couple of truck drivers behind me gestured their annoyance at my low speed, as only truck drivers can do.** Unfortunately my luck ran out before I got to the forecourt, and ran out of fuel. At least I hoped that was the problem. The tank was drained to almost nothing before being crated in Sydney. After walking along the motorway I came to the fuel station and asked to buy a fuel can. I was surprised to find they didn't sell them, but someone found a plastic bottle in a bin and offered it to me. The problem was solved. I returned to the bike, added the fuel, and rode on to the station straight up to the air hose. It wasn't working. The facility existed, but was missing its hose and connector. The guy who had helped find the plastic bottle for me, also went out of his way to find the next solution. He asked a lorry driver who, very obligingly, fitted an air line to his truck's compressor, and pumped up my tyre. He even had a gauge to verify the pressure I required. The kindness of strangers, in my first hour on the road in South America, produced a warm glow inside me, and a huge grin to prove it.

I settled in to Santiago life for a few days. As I was later to discover throughout South America, it had a typical mix of 16th. and 17th. Century Spanish colonial architecture and culture, together with a vibrant modern buzz. I liked that. Spirited street art displayed considerable talent by artists with a wide range of styles. In the Pinochet era 'artists' or political activists risked arrest and imprisonment if they were caught spraying anti-government messages on to the city walls. That period was now in the past, but the street art had been allowed to continue, perhaps even flourish. Strictly speaking it was still illegal, so I was told, but was now tolerated. Tourists seemed to like it so I was sure that helped. It was certainly colourful, and covered up otherwise un-loved walls. I also learnt that it had become quite a competitive activity between local communities, even nearby towns, all trying to create the best new work.

Dictatorships, and a military coup had given way to democracy now, and most people seemed content enough with that. One opinion offered to me was that there was little to choose between the political parties; a view I thought could apply to almost every democracy.

It was not until I got to Chile that I looked at a map of it separately from the continent. It is very long and thin, ranging from the Atacama desert towards the north, to mountains, fjords and glaciers in the south. I headed south.

I met a man called Temis at the first stop. Or rather, he met me, attracted by the bike of course. He was riding a well prepared Suzuki Versys, which looked far more suitable for South American roads than my Rocket. He had been dared by friends to ride from his home town in Colombia to the very bottom of Tierra del Fuego at Ushuaia, the most southerly town in the world, and back again of course. He accepted the dare, and made some stickers for his bike to declare his goal. He gave me one to display next to my 'please stop smoking' message. It bore his name, the names Colombia and Ushuaia, and the Spanish word for dare; *Reto*. The sticker remained on my bike throughout the journey. In fact I later found out that a lot of people ride their adventure in South America using stickers applied to fuel station windows to promote where they have been. A little like the American phrase *'Kilroy was here'*, accompanied by a cartoon, and used extensively in the second world war.

Crossing over the Andes mountains on my second day, I was expecting and hoping for some glorious snow capped scenery. I had made sure all my cold weather gear was to hand, but ended up disappointed. The altitude was hardly a challenge at all and most of the trees were dead. The dry, lifeless passage in to Argentina was only made interesting by the excellence of the lunchtime steak served to me in a modest little cafe. Just when I thought I was the only one venturing into the wilderness alone, a town appeared beside a lake. It had taken some inspiration from the Swiss and imitated chalet designs all along the side of the lake. There were even two dozen new Triumph Tigers in the car park of one of the hotels, apparently there on a tour from Brazil.

By now I was riding along the famous Ruta 40. It runs most of the length of South America, but a little like Route 66 from Chicago to Los Angeles, it was no longer complete. The further south I rode along it, the flatter the landscape became. In Patagonia, the trees became shorter, the bushes became spinier, and the grasses became coarser. For much of the journey there was nothing but grass.

Llamas were the most common animal, often hopping gracefully over the sheep fences to reach tastier grass. I amused myself by noticing the gormless look on their faces. We had many a conversation as I slowed down to ease past them in the road. Strange things went on inside my helmet when there was no one else to talk to. Unlike the kangaroos in the Outback, the Llamas of Patagonia had two brain cells. The second one told them that when they heard the sound of an engine approaching, they should jump away from it. Jumping in any direction, sometimes in to the path of the oncoming vehicle, was the kangaroo reaction. The Llamas froze, stared with a vacant expression, them jumped away from me. Some of them in fact managed to communicate with me. Their look conveyed surprise, a certain amount of cognitive activity, the suggestion of recognition, the realisation that I was approaching, and the decision to run away. I saw remarkably few of them in a decaying heap on the side of the road. Perhaps I should credit them with three brain cells. There were in fact a few more Rhea who did not make it across the road. These were short, grey, emu or ostrich-like flightless birds. Neither animal was particularly obliging to me and my camera. I didn't expect to see many more armadillos crossing the road on my travels, but there were quite a few further south. Very cute.

After two days of this I was getting a little bored. I could speak *'stralian* in Australia, and engage with the people I met. However, my inability to speak Spanish was frustrating me. Of course I learnt how to ask a hotelier the basic question; *"Una habitación y una comida por una noche por favor."* However, that was not a great way to start a real conversation. In fact, there weren't really many people to talk to anyway. Patagonia was quite empty.

I had a big decision ahead about Ruta 40. Should I continue to follow it, even if I knew that it was unpaved ahead? If I detoured, and added a whole day to my plan, I could stick to tarmac. A few bikers suggested I would be OK on gravel, but I met a group on three smaller adventure bikes, each with a man and woman on board, with luggage, who told me they tried but turned back when they got bogged down in soft gravel, and took the detour instead. The question of riding as far as Ushuaia, or not, was a constant thought too. There's nothing much there really except a port and some hotels. There's a photo opportunity with a signpost that confirms you have made it. I would have welcomed that one for the collection but I had another goal in mind. I had already abandoned the fantasy of visiting Antartica. My Rocket would not have got there, or perhaps would not have been allowed to get there. I didn't find out. It would have been too expensive a trip by sea passage from Ushuaia anyway, and would have felt too self indulgent for me.

No, I decided my goal was the Perito Moreno Glacier.

It took me five days riding eight to ten hours a day, to travel from Santiago to the glacier. My direction had been almost exclusively south, but to get there I detoured west a few hundred kilometres short of Ushuaia. This monster of a glacier, thirty kilometres long, slid gracefully down the southern tip of the Andes, ignoring the Chile / Argentina boundary on its way. Eventually it tumbled in to the cloudy light blue abyss of Lake Argentine. As it did so, chunks fell off. Gentle cracking sounds were heard constantly but a louder crack like gunfire indicated the next fall. The sound resonated across the lake and would be followed by rumbling, splashing, and gurgling sounds as another mini iceberg calved away from the ice field. They would sink, bob up, roll, and then force waves to cross the narrowest part of the lake. Yelps from tourists like me, tingled my spine. It was a truly awesome sight and experience; one I had only hoped to see if I was lucky. It transpired that this happened several times a day throughout the summer months. Global warming was not to blame. It had been happening like this for centuries. Summer temperatures were always above freezing, and the lake surface was only one hundred and eighty metres above sea level. As most glaciers retreated, the Perito Moreno was considered unusual as it advanced. It ended its glacial life with inevitability at this point. I was lucky enough to capture a couple of video sequences, and photos, as sections almost seventy-five metres high toppled over.

— — —

It was time to head north. After almost a year of heading south, mostly, I turned around.
Two signposts made life interesting on the way back up. In fact they were both a series of posts.
The first series told me that the Malvinas / Falkland Islands belonged to Argentina.
As a proud British citizen I fully supported my country's decision to send our fleet to recover British sovereign territory after Argentina invaded the Falkland Islands in 1982. Following a chance conversation with an Argentinian diplomat in London

many years later I learnt that Argentina believed that it acquired the islands from Spain when it achieved independence in 1816. However, the UK subsequently expelled Argentinians in 1833 and banned them from future colonisation.
The geographical position of the islands was useful to Britain, helping fishing, whaling, merchant shipping and the Navy. The discovery of offshore oil had complicated issues in more recent years. Seeing the signs again in Patagonia, particularly the ones telling me I was just a few hundred kilometres from the islands, fuelled my curiosity once more. I started to wonder how I would feel if Argentina had settlers on the Isle of Wight, and claimed it belonged to them. How would I feel about that? How would any UK citizen feel about that? The proximity of the Falklands to Argentina, not the UK, should be enough to settle the dispute, shouldn't it?

Notoriously strong winds cross southern Patagonia, and a series of signposts warned me that they were there. I needed no warning as I had already been leaning in to them for several days. However, the signs were amusingly graphic. A tall tree trunk, curving substantially towards the east, was topped with a few upturned branches in the same direction. The result looked more like a warning for Bobby Charlton hair.

I passed the llamas, sheep and rheas again, and eventually skimmed the east coast. This was my first sighting of the Atlantic Ocean for almost a year. I gave a cheer. I felt homeward bound, despite realising there was still a long way to go. It took another couple of days for me to reach Argentina's capital.

Buenos Aires was much larger than Santiago, reflecting the greater prosperity in Argentina, over a longer period. There were many beautiful buildings and statues in a colonial style, as well as art installations, colourfully painted walls, and modern architecture. Eva Peron's image, in neon lights, engulfs a tower block, and Juan Manuel Fangio's brass statue with his F1 car dominates the square in front of the Mercedes building. I noticed quite a few places offering Tango lessons, and, briefly, considered giving it a go. The city hosts two well known football clubs, both with massive stadiums, and a reputation for having particularly passionate supporters. Visiting Club Atletico River Plate and Boca Junior was easy as they were in the middle of town. Unfortunately there were no games scheduled during my time there.

Even in Buenos Aires I saw references to the fact that Argentina still thought that Islas Malvinas / Falkland Islands, belonged to them. Argentina had a couple of other disputes which interested me. They claimed to have invented the Tango, but so did Uruguay. The evidence I read seemed to side with Uruguay, but Argentina popularised and supported it in a way which overwhelmed their smaller neighbour. They also claimed that the Rio Plata (River Silver, not the mistranslated River Plate) was the widest in the world at 137 miles from Buenos Aires over to Montevideo in Uruguay. In the middle of Buenos Aires the fresh water was clear enough to be drawn off and filtered for drinking. Further out, it was too brackish to drink as it was closer to the sea. The debate therefore continued as to whether it was a river or estuary at the widest point. It was certainly wide, that I could tell.

Heading north again the temperature and humidity rose as I crossed the Tropic of Capricorn. I rode in a fairly straight line with the Uruguay border over my right shoulder, and the Paraguay border over my left. Deep into rural north Argentina I realised there were no towns of any size ahead of me, and no hotel signs had appeared for quite a while. In the late afternoon sunshine I eventually spotted the word 'hotel', hand written on the side of a whitewashed barn. I pulled up into the yard and entered the only building that looked like it might be for humans, not animals. A lady took me to a row of four doors and showed me that there was indeed a bedroom and bathroom inside. She told me that she would cook a meal later. Great. That was all I needed. She also pointed out that just outside my door a new aerial had been installed which allowed me to watch satellite television. She grabbed the remote control, ran through a couple of channels, and stopped at the pornography option. Suddenly I was uncomfortable, realising that I was standing next to a short, overweight, middle aged lady, not very attractive, in the middle of a remote farm, looking at her watching hard-core pornography. It was still the afternoon.

I agreed to pay the low price she asked and busied myself with the usual bike de-stuffing routine. That was followed by a visit to the bathroom. Whilst doing my ablutions, I noticed the shower curtain was moving slightly. I shook it and four cockroaches fell out. Still with my motorcycle boots on I was able to bring their lives to a swift end. One more cockroach appeared later on the floor beside my bed as I was getting in to it. That one too was dispatched, but in a more James Bond-like tarantula moment in 'Dr. No.' I slept well enough for half the night but was woken by yet another one. This incompetent critter fell on to my head from the beam above. After flicking it to the floor I didn't manage to grab my boot in time before it disappeared. That was the end of my night's sleep. I lay there wondering how the evening had moved from cocks to cockroaches.

On the next two consecutive days I had to double back on myself. The first was to recover my phone which I had managed to leave on the bed of my gloomy room in cockroach hotel. The pornography queen had recovered it and seemed genuinely relieved to be able to hand it back to me. I was relieved too. The second time was to return to the Argentine border which I had shot through ten minutes earlier without remembering to get my Carnet stamped. There was no barrier or guards, but I eventually tracked down a man in an office who had a rubber stamp.

In north Argentina the border with Brazil runs along the course of the River Iguazu, and quite close to the border with Paraguay too. The middle of the river was my next destination. The Iguazu Falls. This is an enormous three kilometre run of about 275 waterfalls, depending on the water level. The drop ranges from 60 to 80 metres. This made it the largest waterfall complex in the world. Tourists entered via a national park. Some elevated paths led everyone right to the very edge of a horseshoe in the middle of the falls. Everybody gets drenched by the warm spray but no-one minds of course because of the exhilaration of the experience. The vast, relentless flow roared as it crashed in to the billowing mist below.

15. Thongs and other things.

Crossing in to Brazil, and riding along, was easy enough. I had pre-translated my Spanish phrase, asking for accommodation, into Portuguese, but couldn't see where to stop and ask. On either side of the larger towns along the main highway, there were buildings marked 'hotel' or 'motel'. However, their design confused me. They had high walls around them, and gates marked in and out, but no windows. Nothing remotely resembled a reception door. The names were a puzzle too, at first. 'Love Hotel', 'Las Vegas Passion Hotel', and 'Motel Intimiso' gave me some clues. They were brothels. Nearer the centre of another town I found an American-style motel. Although it was old and run-down, it fulfilled my need for a night. A guest there spoke a little English and was able to enlighten me about the other motels. He said that although some had prostitutes available, most were for couples to enjoy an evening together. This included young courting couples, illicit extra-marital relationships, or happily married couples just wanting to get away from the children and mother-in-law for a night. No doubt they all wanted to make a bit of a noise. I also learnt that these love hotels provided condoms free of charge, by law. In addition you could order a meal and champagne to be delivered as you would no doubt build up an appetite. Certainly an interesting business model.

I was also puzzled to see quite a few very large brand new warehouses, still obviously empty. I was never able to confirm the reason, but wondered if a commitment to build them when Brazil's economy was doing well had been scuppered by yet another crisis. Certainly there were some exceptionally large and prosperous looking factories bearing some well known names; Toyota, Honda, Carrefour, New Holland, and Johnson & Johnson, amongst many others. So the country was not just about rain forests and football, I thought. The roads were good; not too busy and flowing well. I stopped for lunch at one of the popular churrasceria restaurants, serving excellent steak, cooked on a large skewer and sliced off over my plate. The supply was endless but eventually I realised I had eaten enough red meat for a month. After filling my stomach, and my petrol tank too, I set off again, in the general direction of Sao Paulo. Slipping in to the fast moving traffic I changed up from second to third gear. Or at least I tried to. The engine revved, but did not engage the gear. I tried again and again. After a sickening grinding, crunching sound, it got there. The same thing happened when changing from third to fourth, then again up to fifth. Apart from that it was riding well. Everything else felt good. I changed down to pull in to another forecourt at the next opportunity. It failed to engage again, mostly, but sometimes it seemed to have found a sweet spot. After a thorough visual inspection of the clutch lever, cable, linkage and so on, I could see nothing wrong. The problem had to be within. I decided to chance my luck and ride on.

My Plan A for dealing with a major problem had always been to contact the nearest Triumph dealer. Researching Brazil earlier on I had spotted dealers in both Sao Paulo and Rio de Janeiro. I hoped to get safely as far as Sao Paulo and soon decided that was possible so long as nothing else broke as a consequence of the first problem, whatever that was. Riding along still felt good, but heavier traffic on the outskirts of Sao Paulo had me changing gear uncomfortably often. The high temperature and humidity did not help either, nor too the absence of a hotel sign. It took me two hours of riding a main highway around, through, and almost past the vast city before I found one near an airport. It was an ingloriously formulaic type of airport hotel, but at least it had a room for me. I ordered a bowl of chicken soup through room service which turned out to be quite good, and my mood improved. A thought had been growing which now needed a decision to be made. Another one that was typical of the many decisions necessary to complete a journey around the world. Sao Paulo looked energetic, successful and crowded, but seemed to have little to offer a tourist except for a few historic colonial buildings and plazas. I had seen quite a few of them already in South America. The thought of waiting here whilst my bike was fixed by Triumph did not really appeal to me. Of course I had no idea what was wrong, or if it could be fixed promptly. It might take weeks. The prospect of waiting for that to happen in Rio de

Janeiro was a lot more appealing. I sent an email to Triumph Rio, and hoped for the best.

A reply was despatched early the following morning from Triumph's marketing manager. Erika promised me prompt attention and wished me a safe ride directly to their service department.

The whole team at Triumph Rio Barra could not have been more pleased to see me. They enthused over my journey, my beast, and myself. We talked energetically about London, Hinckley in Leicestershire where Triumph Rockets were made, and 'For the Ride'. Triumph's on-line magazine had written twice about my journey up to this point. It did not take them long at all to find the cause of the problem. A spring had broken. That was all. It was a chunky one, and importantly connected my selected gear with the transmission. After eight years of riding Triumph Rockets, this was the first part that had 'broken'. My unbreakable beast had finally shown me it was only human after all.

Triumph apologised for the fact that the new spring might take a few days to arrive, and as those days spanned the Easter weekend it might take even longer. I was delighted by the news of a delay, as well as a solution, and was already looking forward to spending time in Rio. There really could not have been a better place for me to relax. I headed for a hotel in Copacabana, and the beach.

Beach life in Rio was quite different to beach life in Europe. The people of Rio are called *'Cariocas'*. Unless you learn their behaviour and follow it, you stand no chance of blending in. There were a set of unwritten rules to be learnt and followed. On arrival you have to choose your spot carefully. Not too close to the shore as every now and then a Trans-Atlantic wave would carry away your towel and beach bag. Not too near the famous Copacabana promenade as the scorching sun would bake your feet on your way from your towel to the sea. And not somewhere in between either because that was where Cariocas played games. *Frescobol* was played with a wooden racquet and a hard ball. *Pelada* was basically football with fewer players and improvised goal posts just a couple of feet apart. *Futevolie* was a bigger game involving feet and hands. There's beach volleyball too played nearer the top of the beach with a net and court lines in the sand. All of these games seemed to be taken very seriously. I was captivated by a group of young ladies one day who were playing *'keepie uppie'* - the art of keeping a football in the air whilst only using their feet, ankles, knees, chest, shoulders and head, and then passing it on to another player, again without letting the ball fall. They were very skilful. If all of that activity wasn't enough of a test for me, avoiding sand being flicked in my face, I then had to find the best spot to establish my umbrella. This too seemed to be an art form for Cariocas. First you thrust the spiked end in to the ground, and rotated it in a clockwise direction, before adding the parasol top half and hoping that you had judged the angle of the sun well enough to cover your chosen ground. Then, and I watched this many times, they would scoop out a hole, using just one foot, and create a mound to rest their upper body. The lady in the party would then unwind her *kanga* (beach shawl) from around her waist, lay it over the dugout, and settle in to position to watch everybody else doing the same. They would often stand up again, adjust their *tanga* (thong bikini), and settle down again. The men would generally run in to the sea and dive or flip without hesitating. After a swim they would return to pick up a surf board or body board known as *bodibodin*, and terrify every one else by their speed in the crowded water.

Chilled beer vendors occupied important positions along the beach and I was assured that every Carioca had their favourite bar. No one went hungry either as an endless stream of sandwiches, snacks and something tasteless called *biscotto de polvilho* were paraded up and down all day long. In amongst these salesmen were scruffier looking men, who were not there to sell something, but to steal. A careless lapse of concentration was all these people needed to relieve me of something valuable, I was told.

On slightly quieter weekdays, often around lunchtime, people would arrive in their swim wear under a loose pair of shorts and t-shirt, and ask someone, a stranger, to guard their bag, presumably containing money, wallet, watch and perhaps car keys too, whilst they had a swim. Afterwards they would stand near the water's edge and dry themselves in the sun and sea breeze. To my uneducated eye the use of a beach towel seemed to be optional. On my last day though I was finally chosen to be someone's bag guardian. I felt like I had a chance of becoming a Carioca.

My decision, tens of thousands of miles back, not to spend time alone on a beach again, was willingly tossed aside for the beaches of Rio. In fact I had quite forgotten that decision as I rushed across the famous portuguese pavement waves on my first day, lured, I fully admit, by thongs (tanga). Very un-European-like, almost every lady wore thongs. Curvacious, suntanned bottoms were everywhere, but top-less bathing was not permitted.
Many of my days on the beach ended with a lengthy stroll along the esplanade where tables would be hastily erected for just an hour to create Rio's famous cocktail called *Caipirinha*. Limes and sugar were crushed together and mixed with a spirit called *cachaca* made from sugar cane. Different strengths and qualities of *cachaca* were available and all had to be tried. Truly a perfect end to a tough day on a beach.

Coastal mountains and granite outcrops added a unique feel to the city, and served to separate neighbourhoods. Between them all life existed: luxury apartments, simpler tower blocks, shopping malls, businesses and shops, restaurants and bars. All seemed seamlessly connected to the promenade and beach, particularly as they were all on the same level. Almost every street corner had its own bar / coffee shop called a *boteco*. Locals were known by name and their individual preferences were well served. I was not there long enough to be well known, but after the first week my mid-morning coffee was served to me on arrival at the nearest one to my hotel, without having to ask for it.

Seven hundred metres above the city on Corcovado mountain, stands the statue of "Christ the Redeemer". The reinforced concrete and soapstone structure was thirty meters tall and twenty-eight meters wide. This beguiling figure was now listed as one of the Seven New Wonders of the World. He had a great view from up there, but my favourite overlook was from the top of Sugar Loaf Mountain. Its name refers to the shape of the refined sugar cones that were exported to Portugal in colonial times, but latter-day tourists were taken to its summit by cable car. The view from there allowed me to look back on the Central, South, and North zones of the city. The lush green granite minimountains contrasted with the sparkling white and grey buildings between them. The sandy beaches stood out from the marinas, and the rhythm of the city seemed tangible even from my high viewing point. Corcovado was in the distance but Christ and I still had a clear view of each other. I felt sure that he gave me half a smile, with a raised eyebrow.

After a week I was falling in love with Rio. Everything about it was appealing to me. The further I ventured from my hotel walking in ever increasing circles, the more I appreciated it. I was no longer thinking about my bike's broken spring as a disappointment, but a stroke of luck.

It was time for football again as, with luck on my side, there were games on at the world famous Maracana stadium. It was the largest in Brazil and had hosted two World Cup Finals and the Olympic Games. Cariocas take their football very seriously and all support one of a choice of four premier division teams based in Rio. Flamengo and Botofago had played each other the evening before. It was a Carioca Cup semi final. One supporter didn't get to see the game as he was killed in a crowd scuffle outside the ground even before it had started. I was glad I didn't learn that until afterwards. My game was between Vasco da Gama and Fluminense. Fans sat in either the north or south stands to make the most noise together, singing their chants and banging their drums. I chose to sit mid way between, overlooking the half-way line. Opposing supporters sat happily next to each other and when either team scored I was surprised to be caught up in a frenzied multi-hug with everyone around me, irrespective of allegiance. At two all the game got a little fractious so the referee kept adding extra time. Eventually Vasco scored a winner in the 97th minute, and half the crowd went home feeling as if the evening had changed their lives for the better. The glorious game was on quite another level in Brazil.

Other crowded houses clung to the steepest hills in Rio; the favelas. These were illegally constructed dwellings, or slums, with a fearsome reputation for unregulated living. They didn't distress me at all, despite twice hearing gun shots from the one closest to my hotel. The hotel staff said they were just having fun firing in to the air, but I imagined that was their reassuring response whenever a tourist asked. In fact they were less of a threat than they used to be. The city council had made a huge effort in recent years to stabilise them. Many now had mains services installed including water and electricity. There were paved streets with lighting, and police stations in amongst them. They were not built to enjoy the view but I couldn't help wondering what it might be like.

The favelas and the people who lived there, the homeless living in the streets near the beach, the thieves walking the beaches looking for opportunities, all served to give the city an uneasy edge, which I liked. To me they represented the reality of modern city living, earning a certain amount of sympathy, and reminding the rest of us of our good fortune. I could not say that the fortunate and unfortunate were happy living together side by side, but they were at least living together.

Triumph Rio Barra called to say the spring had been fitted and all was well. They had also cleaned and polished the Rocket X to look like new, and declined to accept payment from me. Thank you Triumph Brazil.

I headed west for a while, almost back to Sao Paulo initially, then north-west towards the border with Bolivia. Brazil continued to impress me with the obvious size of its economy, based on agriculture and industry, but otherwise seemed full of people just getting on with their lives. After a couple of days I was at the border, registering my exit from Brazil, and looking forward to new experiences. Unfortunately, as soon as I entered Bolivia I wanted to leave.

The smiles were worth more than a bribe. Java, Indonesia.

Upstaged on Bali, Indonesia.

Reflecting on the moment. New Zealand.

A bungy jump in full leathers. Why not?

Half way around my world.

The Australian Outback is full of life, I promise.

Daily entertainment at the Perito Moreno Glacier, Argentina.

Iguazu Falls, Argentina / Brazil Border.

I could feel the rhythm of Rio from the top of Sugar Loaf Mountain, Rio de Janeiro, Brazil.

Ruta 7 blocked on the road to nowhere. Bolivia.

The Uros tribe on Lake Titicaca, Peru / Bolivia.

Remarkable stonework holds Machu Picchu together, Peru.

The simplest of pleasures kept me entertained in Lima, Peru.
Bagels, cream cheese and avocados.

Fishing on the Amazon, Peru. I caught this Piranha, then ate it
for lunch.

Sugar cane convoy in Colombia.

'World Famous'

'Undocumented alien' entering the USA.

Jasper and Banff National Park, Canada.

16. No money for a teacher.

The border leaving Brazil was different to most I had experienced as it lacked the usual line of trucks belching diesel fumes in my face. It did however have the usual row of cars loaded with family members and bags, and the odd crate of chickens. There were Brazilians travelling out, and Bolivian travelling in. Occasionally one would be stopped for a token inspection but most were simply waved through.

Foreigners on motorbikes were unusual. I presented my paperwork and was told I needed to have two copies of the entry form. I didn't have two copies, and didn't have a photocopy machine on my bike either. Their copier had stopped working and the man who might be able to get it going again was at lunch. The wait was not much fun but eventually I was able to proceed. Feeling relieved, I rode around the corner towards the no-man's land that usually accompanies border posts, and could scarcely believe what I saw. An expanse of compacted mud and craters greeted me. I wondered if I had taken a wrong turn and lost the road, but the steady stream of those cars and chickens were making their way through. We all chicaned our way around the holes, crossing from one side to the other looking for a safe path. It only took a few minutes though before I arrived at the entry point in to Bolivia but was again staggered by the post-apocalyptic scene. The offices were crumbling, windowless, doorless and almost roofless. I slowed to a crawl to see where I needed to present my passport but there was no-one in sight. The scruffy little town just beyond seemed to confirm I was indeed in Bolivia. A lady at a table in front of her little shop waved at me from the other side of the road. I shouted *"Cambio?"* at her and she beckoned me over.

As always with every new country I had checked exchange rates on line before arrival. My remaining Brazilian Reals were converted to Bolivian Bolivianos at a remarkably good rate. She even walked me to an ATM to withdraw some more. I bought a cup of coffee and snack from her, and rode on.

The roads weren't too bad, at first, but broke up a little as I progressed. The first surprise were the Mennonites. They all travelled together in covered carts pulled by horses, slipping in and out of well cultivated fields. I later learnt that they were known as Russian Mennonites, but Bolivia had permitted numbers to swell from other European nations.

The sun was fading as I stopped in consecutive little towns to search for a hotel, without success. The next one appeared ahead, attractively called Carmen. I was determined to find a bed there, and not risk riding any further in the fading light. Pulling off the main road the first residents to greet me were the wild dogs. They ganged up against me and snapped at my heels as I ventured on. Sand had blown in to town and was piled up in shallow drifts along the streets. There were not many buildings and even fewer people, but eventually a town square appeared. In my best Spanish I asked several people where I could find a room and meal. I rode up and down the street I was directed to, before eventually spotting a light above a barbecue with a solitary chicken roasting in it. Beyond the light were a couple of plastic tables and chairs. This, apparently, was my hotel for the night. The family were very friendly and showed me to a row of doors in their back yard. They offered me a choice, with or without air conditioning, and seemed particularly pleased with my choice. I agreed to pay the asking price equivalent to nine pounds sterling. The chicken meal later, served with rice, salad, and a drink, cost me ninety pence. However, the proprietor's idea of what constituted air conditioning, and mine, turned out to be quite different. The bathroom had a flushing toilet, not bad, and a single plastic pipe above it in the middle of the ceiling. Either on or off, without a shower head, this was indeed the shower. The basin, for brushing my teeth, was out in the yard guarded by more wild dogs.

A wry smile was on my face in the morning as I took a coffee and bread with the family. I had survived the night, of course I had, and I was now enjoying their company, recognising the vast differences between their home and mine. The children were healthy and happy, and loved playing on my bike. Another cherished photo was captured with two of them on the seat.

As I pulled away and out of the town I was again taken by surprise. There were groups of children, all in smart uniforms, happily making their way to a colourful new school around the next corner.

Throughout much of South America I had come across Police check points on a regular basis. Those who stopped me were shown my Passport and bike registration details. It was no surprise therefore that Bolivia did the same. The first of these was not long into my ride out of the not so attractive Carmen. I was pulled over and showed my Passport. The officer took it but didn't open it. He rubbed his finger and thumb together to indicate he wanted me to pay a bribe. I refused and raised my shoulders to ask why. Everybody else was stopped and handed over a note or two before being allowed to continue. The truck drivers were being asked for paperwork and after a noisy exchange of opinions, they too handed over some money. I stood my ground and was then taken by the sergeant in to his hut. It was small and crammed with people handing over money. He repeated the forefinger and thumb gesture and I repeated my refusal. I had not been asked to show my bike paperwork, and gestured that it was all in order and in my top box. The sergeant responded by half opening the drawer under his desk and showing me the contents. It was stuffed full of money. My heart pounded a little faster as I continued to refuse him. I had done nothing wrong. I opened my palm and asked for my Passport. It took a few attempts but he eventually handed it back to me, too busy to bother with me whilst dealing with the stream of money coming his way from others. The whole process of collecting money was so blatant that I later reflected on whether or not I had mis-understood it. There had been no-one controlling my entry in to Bolivia the day before so perhaps this check point was part of their process. I was to have to wait until I left Bolivia before learning what should have happened.

I followed Ruta 7 for another day towards Bolivia's largest city, Santa Cruz de la Sierra. It occupied flat land east of the Andes, and also boasted a Triumph dealer. The road had been not terribly interesting so I switched to Ruta 4 to climb the mountain range towards the capital. It also seemed to be more direct than Ruta 7 though both would get me to La Paz eventually.

Santa Cruz had a plethora of vicious speed humps, many too high for me to slip over without grinding my sump on them. Others had not been maintained, or perhaps had been vandalised by locals. There would often be nothing much left of them except a terrifying row of steel bolts for me to work my way around at the last minute. The towns on the outskirts of the city had the same hurdles. Continuing west I passed about half a dozen smaller communities before they eventually stopped troubling me. Relaxing for a while, enjoying the mountain views, twisting roads, lush vegetation and children waving at me as always, I came to a grinding halt. The traffic was stationary. I rode carefully past about a hundred cars and trucks before reaching the head of the line. A crowd gathered around some piles of soil, a few rocks, some tree branches, lots of rope, and some home made banners. On the other side were a bunch of men, looking determined to stay in position. A couple of them let off home made fireworks; rockets. They screamed in to the air and reverberated off the sides of the narrow valley. Women sat on the side of the road, under a little shelter. I approached the first rope but was unable to work out the problem. In due course, recognising my number plate, a Frenchman living in Bolivia explained the issue. Apparently these sort of protests were common. This one was about the school in the village ahead. Funding had been made available to build it, but there was no money left to employ a teacher. Powerless on their own, the protesters felt they needed to draw attention to their plight. I was sympathetic, for a while, and decided to wait patiently. I was told the road block would be opened at midday, and we could all go on our way. Twelve o'clock came and went, and there was nowhere left to shelter from the sun. I approached the rope once more and made pleading motions with the man who appeared to be a leader, about my age. He shook his head from side to side. I backed away, but returned later a little less patient. I threatened to pull the rope aside and gestured that all I wanted was a narrow path through the middle. In fact I would have had to persuade them to move a tree trunk and flatten a pile of earth as well. A younger man stepped forward to show me he had a machete in his hand. Simultaneously, I decided to step back just as the older man stepped forward to calm the younger man. I felt quite invincible in my full leather suit at times. However, it wasn't difficult to conclude that I had better take off my jacket, calm down, and re-consider the day. Just then, an old lady appeared from the village carrying a cool box full of home made ice cream. I bought one with an extra large cone. The flavour was indiscernible, but sweet and icy. It went down very well. One o'clock came and went. Some in the line had turned back and given up. I was considering doing the same, especially as the Frenchman had done so leaving me without a friend to interpret what was happening. But at two o'clock they sounded an air horn and swiftly got to work removing their barricade. They did so with an efficiency and manner which suggested to me that this was a common routine for them.

The afternoon progressed well enough for a while before I hit road works. My side of the road had a man controlling traffic with a red-for-stop and green-for-go sign. A little further ahead it was the other side of the road that was being re-laid. A little after that it was both sides at the same time. The road narrowed as it climbed, and deteriorated further. There were more complications ahead with streams crossing the unmade road, equipment left rusting, and the odd bridge reduced to just one lane. A group of yellow jacketed construction team members were working scarily close to the edge of a gushing torrent, directing one vehicle at a time over their new reinforced concrete bridge, still only with one lane, and no barrier to hold me back if I slipped on its already muddy surface. Just when I started to wish for an easier passage I encountered a four by four warning of an oversized load coming towards me. It was certainly oversized but on the narrow, twisting, wet, unmade, jungle road it seemed colossal. I had to pull over with my right boot resting against a rock to allow it to pass. The labels on the side told me it was made in China. It was a tall, wide, grey, steel rectangular structure with three covered holes at the front. Quite why it was there, or where it was going I never figured out. To my utter dismay it was followed by five more identical loads, spaced apart. From China they must have crossed the Pacific, entered Chile, and traveled by road to this point. Only a little further on I turned a corner and ground to an unstable halt in soft shingle. I couldn't go forward and struggled to push backwards but eventually got clear after dismounting. The straight hill ahead had the same loose shingle on my side of the road, and piles of a coarse sand and soil mix on the other side. I walked up the hill but there was no sign of any improvement. Peering around the next corner I could see more construction traffic and yet more hills disappearing over the horizon. I walked back down the hill to my bike and was close to the obvious decision. My mind was made up as a construction plough appeared behind me and flattened the sand piles over both sides of the road. I had to turn back. I not only couldn't get up the hill, but saw nothing ahead to encourage me to keep going.

I descended, and slipped gingerly past the six Chinese structures, which had now come to a halt. There was no way they were going to get over the new single lane bridge. I left them to it, and continued on, passing the road block village, and eventually to the steel stud section again. The day was drawing to an end but I felt sure that I had spotted a hotel sign somewhere along there. The only one I found displayed its five star status. It was an extraordinary adventure, climbing a long and winding private road to the reception. Apart from in the very centre of Santa Cruz, I had seen nothing but poverty in Bolivia to this point. My mind was running at full speed trying to work out how this place might be viable. Corruption, politicians or drug money was the only conclusion I came to. I had little choice but to stay, and was grateful for the fact that the room was not too expensive. Even more bizarrely, I soon realised that I was the only guest staying there. The whole enormous development was eerily empty. The evening meal was a tender steak, but even after arranging a time for breakfast with the waiter, the morning dawned with locked doors everywhere and not a soul in sight except for the largest beetle I had ever seen, taking an early swim across the pool.
Bolivia was doing its best to baffle me, I thought, and as I rode along back across the studs in the road. I pulled over for a coffee and bread, as well as some fuel. Filling up my tank the day before was an experience with an unusual first, as my number plate had been recorded on a chart. This particular fuel station I pulled in to now was trying to record my number plate on a

computer in the forecourt. The lad was struggling with my letter, number, letter combination so I typed it in myself. Then a drop-box obliged me to record my country. I looked under E for England, U for United Kingdom, B for Britain, G for Great Britain and so on but couldn't find it. In the end I clicked Brazil, and was allowed a full tank. The lad returned with a receipt displaying a demand for payment about two and a half times the amount shown on the pump. Even the inflated price was not expensive, but I refused to pay, and repeatedly pointed at the pump. I was not going to allow them to rip me off, so I sat down a on a chair nearby, and left my bike in situ. The man I had met on my first day riding in South America, Temis, who fulfilled his goal of riding to Ushuia and back to Colombia, told me of a similar difficulty some friends of his had experienced in Bolivia. They had been refused fuel, and were unable to move on until they persuaded a local driver to buy it for them, with an appropriate margin added. Eventually I conceded, paid, and left still wondering why the process of buying fuel was so difficult. My inability to speak any Spanish probably did not help.

Back at the junction where I made the previous day's decision to take Ruta 7, I re-joined Ruta 4. It rode well enough around Santa Cruz, before I hit the first road works. On flatter ground, and heavier traffic, it allowed me to progress, but the day continued with alternating tarmac and gravel sections. As the afternoon turned to early evening I started to look for a town with a hotel. One clue I had noted earlier on was that if a town was large enough to have a hospital or small airstrip, then it was probably large enough to have a hotel. Two consecutive towns failed my usual test. As darkness descended I was determined to succeed in the next town. The main road had nothing to offer, and access to side streets were blocked because road works had reached a 'lets dig a channel deep enough for a new pipe to be laid' phase. Too deep for a Triumph Rocket to pass over. I rode on to the next town, stopped at a brightly lit bank and shouted 'hotel, *habitacion*' at the guard. With a smile and helpful gesture he directed me to the pharmacy next door. Oh well, I thought, I'll ask anyway. A young lady walked me through the stock room to a back yard, where her mother then walked me upstairs, past an open shower area, to a bedroom. At least I thought it was probably a bedroom as it had a bed in it, but nothing else remotely resembling a lettable hotel bedroom. With no choice but to accept her offer, I agreed. She walked me back to the yard and showed me a secure space to park for the night. I slept, but not well as the grill behind the shredded sheet of a curtain was inadequate to allow a flow of air into the stifling room. On a positive note, it was the cheapest night of the trip at the equivalent of a little under £4. The restaurant down the street served a decent meal of chicken, rice, salad and fried potato, as did every other restaurant in Bolivia, washed down with some excellent home made lemonade, served from a bucket.

The following day started with heavy rain, but eased as I climbed the Andes once more, still heading towards the capital, La Paz. I reached a high mountain pass with a classical view. Everything I was expecting to see was there. An arid, treeless landscape with spiny grass, goats and llamas. Ladies with thick woollen yet colourful traditional dress, straw hats over scarves, and a child slung in a blanket on their backs. Dry stone walls separated one field from another, each sheltering a dwelling of stone or brick with a tin roof. Trucks thundered along the highway meandering through the middle of their town. A school had a new basketball court.

The road quality was still good at this point, but soon capitulated. Following a river valley the roadworks started to look very much like the route that had defeated me the day before. Both sides were under construction at the same time, but the surface had at least been compacted by heavy traffic. I bounced, shook and vibrated for longer than I can remember, and eventually reached a sizeable town called Cochabamba. I pulled up in the middle of it, sheltering from the heat under a tree beside a park. It was mid afternoon and I needed to check the map to see if I dared to keep going to La Paz that day, or stay another night en route. As I stepped away from the bike to swig some water, I could immediately see that something didn't look right at the back. All three panniers were now lower than they should have been. The two on either side were now resting on the exhausts, but my tent package under the trunk had prevented that from slipping down too far. The problem was clear.

Bouncing through the mountain road works had caused two of the four bolts holding the luggage assembly together, to shear in two. One of the side panniers had melted slightly, and both exhausts had some of their black paintwork worn away. Nevertheless I was dismayed to realise that two M10 bolts had simply snapped, right by the nut end. I removed the contents, and the side panniers to take a closer look, but decided that the side of a busy road was probably not the best place to continue to attempt a repair. I de-camped to a very conveniently positioned hotel just around the corner. The family running the place were pleased to offer me a secure vehicle space beside their forecourt. Luck was on my side. The broken bolts were easy to remove, and I was carrying a couple of spares with me, left over from when I fitted the luggage set just before leaving London a year earlier. Another problem solved.

I stayed the night and researched both the road ahead and unintentionally the road behind. I was intrigued, or perhaps amused, to learn that earlier in the day I had passed through Chimore. In fact I had stopped for a coffee and snack but not stayed long as two guys hanging around my bike had deep set eyes, dirty clothes, and possibly a problem with a recreational drug. It turned out that Chimore was a centre for cocaine production in Bolivia, allegedly, and was sanctioned by the government.

Setting off again the following morning I had a spring in my step. Moments later it was dashed by the next two fuel stations who refused to serve me. The third one did, and again I helped them out with a country name search on the forecourt computer. More relaxed about their process now, I studied the list calmly. I stopped at the letter R, and exclaimed *Reino Unido*! Spanish for United Kingdom. Of course it was. I knew that, and laughed at my own stupidity for not thinking of it earlier. They charged me the higher price, but by now I had also concluded that this was a kind of road tax for foreign vehicle usage. Fair enough, I thought, so long as the money was actually received by the government. In fact much later on I learnt that the opposite might have been the case. The lower price was subsidised by the government to help its population (and secure votes), and the full price had to be charged to foreign vehicles who were not entitled to the discount.

Ruta 4 continued much as before with tarmac and roadworks alternating constantly. I was growing weary of the effort required just to make progress on Bolivia's roads and looked forward to its junction with Ruta 1, and on to the capital. Bolivia was clearly a poor country and left me with little but sympathy for the daily difficulties facing the population. There was certainly no point in me wishing that my progress through their country could have been easier. Tourism was not a priority for them. Silver mining in previous centuries had brought some prosperity to the country, but the mines were now depleted. Tin, Lithium, natural gas, agriculture and textiles were useful exports but otherwise Bolivia seemed to have little else to offer the world.

Arriving at the start of Ruta 1, the Police officer at the usual check point advised me to ride carefully ahead. I was puzzled, as the route from three major towns merged at this point to start the accent to the capital, about one hundred kilometres further on. There was good tarmac ahead, but it turned out to be a disappointingly short section. Roadworks again! Both sides at once, with nothing but gravel, and very little construction activity, all the way to La Paz.

I was relieved to get there, and was now running low on fuel. Another fuel station turned me down, and the gauge reached zero. The next one turned me down again, but I had had enough. I left the bike at the pump, refusing to move it until they filled me up, and sat down. An earlier decision not to bother with buying a spare fuel can, and keeping it full, might have been about to prove to be the wrong one. Riding from city to city, along main roads, always had places to buy fuel. From the start I had never run too close to running out, though probably had been just about there on a number of occasions. An English speaking motorist assured me that they would serve me eventually if I sat there long enough. However, the manager appeared and politely told me that would not be the case, despite my obvious need and pleading. She returned to her office and emerged a minute later with a Google translate page on her phone to show me. It explained that five kilometres further on there was a fuel station who were authorised to sell fuel to foreign vehicles. She could not do so as the cameras in her forecourt had now recorded my number plate. I expressed gratitude for her assistance and rode on, keeping every finger crossed. Heavy traffic on the outskirts of La Paz slowed me down but miraculously I found the right fuel stop without running out. A smartly dressed, yellow-jacketed supervisor directed me to the right pump, manually recording my number plate. An armed guard then electronically recorded my plate, and accepted my country name, *Reino Unido* of course. I was filled up. Perhaps this level of verification was what was missing at all the previous stops.

I reached my booked hotel in La Paz with the assistance of a couple of enthusiastic bikers who latched on to me at the edge of the city. It was central, of decent quality, and offered a secure car park. I felt a sense of relief to have made it safely this far.
It was a half day ride from La Paz to the border with Peru, so I didn't think there was too much more of an opportunity for Bolivia to throw something else at me. When I entered the country I immediately decided that I wanted to leave. That was still the case, but I was very grateful for all the experiences it had given me.
La Paz itself only interested me for its claim to be the world's highest capital city. At 3,650 metres above sea level it was breathlessly high. I learnt that although the government was based here, the constitutional capital was in fact in Sucre, to the south.

Although my difficulties in Bolivia were troublesome, they were hardly threatening. Nevertheless they helped me come to a conclusion about myself. I was no longer afraid of anything. Or possibly no longer afraid of anything. I was certainly very close to that point. After crossing the Bosphorous in Istanbul, life had constantly thrown me an endless stream of challenges, some of which, in my previous comfortable existence, I would have considered to be dangerous. By the time I reached La Paz I was certainly no longer afraid of guns, gunfire, machetes, border guards, policeman demanding bribes, roads with potholes, unmade roads, running out of fuel, breakdowns, getting lost, cockroaches landing on my head, over congested roads, Indian drivers, empty roads, finding a hotel, finding a lousy hotel, eating anything on offer, and so on. Standing in front of a man striding towards me with a machete in his hand at the road block did not frighten me. It probably should have done. However, his message was clear enough for me to instantly step back to cool the situation down.

17. I love you more than tacos.

A few weeks beforehand I had booked a flight out of Lima, Peru. I was going to meet up with Dalila again. With less than a week to go I realised I was simply not going to get to Lima in time for the flight, and I couldn't cancel. There was a flight leaving La Paz at two o'clock in the morning which would get me to Lima in time to connect with my booking, but the return option would force me to transit via Miami, USA and later sit in Lima airport for 27 hours. It was a ghastly prospect, but there was no alternative but to accept it. I borrowed a redundant suitcase from the hotel front desk, missing its handle, and paid the car park security desk to keep a special eye on my beast whilst I was away.

My destination was Tulum, Mexico, via Cancun airport at the top end of the Yucatan peninsular, and my flight was due to arrive about three hours before Dalila's flight arrived from Lyon. Perfect.

Cancun wasn't the safest place in the world at this time. The city centre had been blighted by a drug trafficking war between rival gangs, leading to hundreds of bloody deaths. Tourists were not being targeted but I was unable to determine whether or not any had been caught up by mistake. Nevertheless, it transpired that one of measures taken to ameliorate the problem was to remove the ability for the traffickers to communicate using wi-fi in and around the airport. So I couldn't contact Dalila. Her terminal was different to mine but when I got there an armed guard prevented me from entering the arrivals area. I could see beyond him that there was an Arrivals board, but it was too far away to read. I could also see that beyond the board everyone arriving was directed to their left towards an enclosed area for taxis, hotel and tour bus pick ups. Dalila would be obliged to follow them, and miss me. Eventually I persuaded the guard to allow me through to read the board, provided that I returned immediately to him. Dalila's flight had just landed, and of course I retuned to the guard as arranged. I think he must have realised that the position he was obliged to patrol was unworkable for arriving passengers to meet up with individuals to greet them, and not wanting a taxi or tour bus. It was a mess. An English speaking Mexican was waiting with me, and faced the same predicament. However, he had been working on a solution and invited me to follow him. There was a side gate to the enclosed taxi area, with an armed guard of course. He negotiated entry for us both for a remarkably small fee. We were in.

I slithered past the arriving crowds and tried to remain inconspicuous in a doorway, until, at last, Dalila appeared. Neither of us could contain our joy, rushing towards each other, screaming and embracing. I was past caring whether or not a guard might be looking for me. We chatted frantically whilst passing one guard after another, exiting at the first guarded barrier that had stopped me. I didn't dare look the guard the eye, but just kept going. We headed towards the office of the car rental company where I had a reservation. On line the reservation price was one of the lowest I had ever encountered, but assumed that was how it was in Mexico. This was my first visit. However, after insurance and other fees were added at the desk, the price almost quadrupled. I lost my temper, cancelled the reservation, stormed off to get a taxi, and concluded that the whole Cancun airport experience had not been a good one.

The ride to Tulum took an hour and a half. Plenty of time for us both to relax.

— — —

Dalila's next prepared question was spectacular. It ran along a similar line to the one she had prepared for me on arrival at Malaga airport the previous summer. The one when she enquired "Mark, is there a question you are planning to ask me?", which led immediately to our engagement. The question this time was on the same theme, but bigger.

"Mark, do you know it is really easy to get married in Mexico?"

I didn't, but replied calmly, and without hesitation this time. "No I didn't know that Dalila, but if it is, let's do it!"

That was all it took for the decision to be made. She told me that she had learnt that Ike and Tina Turner had married in Mexico in 1962. There were others too, many more in fact, right up to the present day. She thought the idea was very romantic, and I was happy to agree. After a good nights' sleep we discussed, and re-confirmed, that was what we wanted to do. We tossed aside the condition in my marriage proposal the previous summer that we should wait until after I had completed my journey, still about five or six months away. There was a practical reason for marrying now too. Dalila had found out that France had lengthy procedures in place for accepting me as a resident following a marriage. The sooner she could start that process the better. We enquired at our hotel reception, who told us where to find the *Registro Civil* in the middle of Tulum, a few minutes away. This was where all civil marriages took place, and all births and deaths were recorded. We strolled in, unannounced, and explained as best we could what we wanted to do. They were as helpful as they could be, but our inability to speak their language left us hoping, rather than knowing, what the procedure would be. Two foreigners marrying in Mexico have a different set of rules than two Mexicans, or one Mexican and one foreigner. Nevertheless we managed to set a date, and wrote it down to confirm.

Step one was to get a blood test and we were duly given a form to present to a nearby laboratory. Blood was taken and the fee paid. Twenty four hours later we had a certificate to prove that we were not using illegal drugs, nor carrying HIV. Back at the *Registro Civil* we learnt about the next step which was to go to a bank to withdraw cash, then to the Town Hall, with another form, to pay the marriage fee in cash, then go back to the *Registro Civil* to prove we had done it. After that the next step was to fill in the marriage application form with basic details like passport number, date of birth and name of parents, as well as give the names of four people to witness the happy moment. Back at our delightful little hotel all the management and staff were by now getting excited about our marriage plans. When we asked them, the first four did not hesitate to agree to be there for us, and witness the ceremony. They entered their names and addresses on the form, which we duly presented back at the *Registro Civil*, once more. There were smiles all round, and the date was re-confirmed.

— — —

Tulum itself was a delightful surprise, with a rough, self-developed feel about it. Our hotel had a recent upgrade, as had others around town, retaining its original character and charming gardens, together with modernities to match client expectations. The town had a good choice of restaurants and shops, all with an independent feel. There were no international hotel chains in sight, which suited us well. The beach was a short hotel-provided bicycle ride away. The sand, palm trees, beach bars and ambiance was very much of the Caribbean. In our first dip in the sea, being the child that I am at heart, I repeated the "Jaws" swimming routine and film score that brought such a smile to our faces on earlier beach holidays. It progressed and quickened, as before, to the chorus of Frankie Valli's "Can't take my eyes off you", with "I love you baby, and if it's quite alright, I need you baby....."
In fact, our hotel pool area and outdoor restaurant played a range of music very much in keeping with our own tastes. It included a song which was new to us. By Carne Cruda, it had a rhythmical Mexican beat, but hilarious lyrics. I couldn't help repeating the title to Dalila; *"I love you more than tacos"*.
We alternated beach trips, and time around the pool, with a quite unique selection of culture and nature experiences. Top of the to-do list was the Mayan township of Chichen Itza. Just over 1000 years old, it was interesting enough to visit, but did not really impress us. In the centre of the development was a pyramid shaped stone structure, with steps up to a temple, used for worship as well as the odd sacrifice. By comparison with the pyramids in Egypt I am afraid I thought it was rather pathetic. As with "Christ the Redeemer" in Rio, it had made its way on to the "Seven New Wonders of the World" list. Perhaps a little bit of vote rigging had got it there. Of much more interest was a larger

area of similar Mayan structures at Coba. Jungle had overwhelmed it and helped to create a more credible atmosphere. It was not beyond our imaginations to feel a connection to the culture of the people who lived there.

Tulum had its own 900 year old archeological site. It was the only Maya city built on the coast, and specialised in trading turquoise and jade.

A little to the south we enjoyed a boat trip through Sian Ka'an, a biosphere reserve. Promises of possible sitings of crocodiles, manatees, turtles and dolphins were all fulfilled.

A visit to the nearby resort of Playa del Carmen was disappointing, but an exhibition on the extraordinary life of artist Frida Kahlo made the day, as did the espresso taken in a coffee shop owned by the son of Bob Marley.

The Yucatan peninsula had extraordinary geography. Fresh water running down from the mountainous hinterland had run over the limestone coastal region and eventually eroded holes in to it. These were known as Cenotes. Inland, some had formed enormous caverns leaving freshwater pools of varying levels at the bottom of them. We visited one called Il Kil. Descending down man made steps through the rock, and around a corner, we were faced with daylight pouring vertically downwards into a black water pool. After our eyes had adjusted to the darkness we could see that others were swimming in it, so we jumped in too. It was fresh and warm; a really enjoyable afternoon.

Another Cenote at Kaan Luum was a completely different experience. Snaking through a mangrove swamp, a muddy path led us on to a creaking wooden jetty and out into a bright salt water lagoon. Below us was a shallow pool over spotlessly clean, almost white sand. Ahead, a deep blue circle came in to view below the surface. This was an offshore Cenote. In a series of short swims, walking in the shallow water squidging sand between our toes, and sunbathing on the jetty, this little piece of paradise felt idyllically tranquil to us.

———

We were casually enjoying a little souvenir shopping on the main street one morning and diverted to the *Registro Civil* to confirm that everything was still good for our marriage the day after. It was just a courtesy visit but their response was catastrophic. Two red faces hiding behind desks shook their heads. There was no reservation for us the following day. In fact, there was no reservation for us at all. After a good deal of paper shuffling and whispers they tried to explain that we had not completed the booking procedure and had not confirmed the date. Dalila hit the roof, and I followed. There were tears. Even after just a short time in Mexico we had learnt from frustrated expats that Mexican authorities had a very annoying habit of only revealing processes one step and a time. That seemed to be what had happened to us. There was one more step to follow. Although our booking form was complete, we needed to present the national ID cards of each witness so that the office could take a photocopy. This had not been explained to us. If it had, then we had misunderstood. We could not be certain which was the case. I tried to understand, and pleaded for them to help us make this happen, but to no avail. Dalila had stormed off by now, very upset, but I didn't follow until a few minutes later. I walked in a daze after her, trying to figure out how this fuck up could have happened. The paperwork was still in my hand when I caught up with her under the shade of a tree. She demanded to know why I hadn't torn it up and thrown it in their faces. That seemed like a pretty good idea to me but I shot back to the office with a different plan. I intended to offer them an extra fee, a bribe blatantly, in order to make space for us on their list. Stepping back in to the office I immediately noticed that the previously empty desk on the left was now occupied. During earlier conversations the red faced team there had referred to a 'Judge' and repeatedly indicated that this was her desk. I approached respectfully, introduced myself, and asked if she spoke English. She indicated 'a little', and smiled. I calmly explained what had happened. She spoke with a member of her team, and referred to a ledger. In due course she offered me a slot in early May, but I repeated that we had a flight booked to leave Cancun on 30th. April. She referred again to the ledger and retuned with a smile. A big one in fact. She would fit us in at ten o'clock on the morning of Monday 30th. April. I shot out to rejoin Dalila and immediately explained that we could go ahead, provided we returned within two hours, when the office closed for the weekend, to present the ID cards of each of our witnesses. Three of them were already at the hotel, and we were soon able to arrange for the fourth to be there in time. We hurtled back to the *Registro Civil*, handed over all four ID cards for photocopying, and confirmed absolutely, without any doubt, that the marriage could go ahead at ten o'clock on the morning of 30th. April. That gave us just two hours for the service and a glass of champagne, before we had to leave Tulum to catch our flights.

Dalila spent the Saturday before the wedding phoning and texting all her family and close friends to announce excitedly what was about to happen. They were all thrilled by the news. It was my turn to call my family on the Sunday but I feared a different reaction. By good fortune, I thought, many of them had gathered together to celebrate a family birthday. I phoned and after speaking to everybody, and offering my best wishes for the birthday, I then announced my happy news. The phone was slammed down on me, with some expletives being screamed in the background. They were still grieving for Sue, even though it had been sixteen months since she passed away. I also had to accept the fact that they had never met Dalila, and I had decided to marry her without them being present.

I was bitterly disappointed in their reaction, but remained determined not to fall out with them. Clearly I still had some bridge rebuilding ahead of me.

Of some comfort, a few hours later, two of my nieces sent messages of congratulations. I shall forever be grateful to them for being the first to do so.

— — —

Our marriage day dawned, like all marriages, with a mix of excitement and anxiety. Coffee, juice, and a hearty Mexican breakfast went down well, presented perfectly as always by our hotel's independent restaurant, Paloma at Coco Hacienda.

Dalila had bought a beautiful pink dress and hat; the hotel gave her a bouquet to carry. Most importantly, the *Registro Civil* was expecting us. All four witnesses arrived promptly, and a fifth member of the hotel team joined us too. The Judge read a couple of sentences in Spanish, then repeated to us in English. We were asked to confirm the contents of the application form and sign it. She then invited us to kiss each other. That was it; we were married!

We didn't expect the ceremony itself to feel romantic, held as it was in the space in front of a desk in a tiny office. However, back at our hotel, truly great guacamole was served, and washed down with ice cold champagne. Huge smiles, genuine congratulations, warm kisses, as well as our considerable gratitude, soon filled the reception with joy.

Our taxi arrived on time. Two hours later we were due to be at the airport; four hours later we were due to be separated.

Possibly the champagne helped the mood, but as we were driven along the remarkably straight and boring road, we seemed to be floating. There was a calmness about us, an utter contentment. The relief was palpable. Marrying in Mexico had not been as easy Dalila believed, but nevertheless achieved, despite some mis-communications.
Feeling as one, we wrapped ourselves in each other's arms and slept a little. Awaking at the departures drop-off area, a ghastly, sinking feeling suddenly gripped us, as we realised we had left a bag behind at the hotel. The one with our new marriage certificate in it. The curse of Cancun airport had struck us again. Calmly, our quick thinking taxi driver phoned and arranged for a second taxi to bring us the bag, driving with a little extra speed to complete the task. Meanwhile, as my flight back to Bolivia was scheduled to leave before Dalila's flight to France, I went to check in first. Without the slightest hesitation, the process was brought to an abrupt halt, and I was refused. I knew that I would be transiting via Miami, and I knew that I did not have a current visa-waiver to enter the US. However, as I was only transiting I would not need one. So I thought. But I was wrong. I was told I

had to have a visa waiver for USA, even if I was only transiting. The curse of Cancun airport had delivered another blow.

My solution might lie at a different airline's sales desk, but that was in another terminal. Leaving Dalila where she was, I hurried over there, using the airport inter-terminal bus service, which was in not so much of a hurry. The first desk offered me the next flight out, not via the US, but with a $12,000 price tag. I turned it down. After a few more enquiries I found a flight the following day, for an acceptable price even though I had lost the fare I had already paid, and remarkably it would still enable me to dove-tail with the Lima to La Paz flight that I had booked a long way back. By the time I got back to Dalila, she had checked in, and passed through passport and security. She had gone. I slumped to the ground against a wall, and sobbed. This wasn't how our marriage was supposed to have started.

I had an awful feeling that the curse would strike again as I tried to find a hotel for the night. It did. After another fruitless airport terminal transport bus ride, to a hotel finder service which was not open, I eventually accepted an offer from a taxi driver, who's 'friend' in town had a room. The hotel, inevitably, was right in the middle of the central hotel zone, where all the drug trafficking murders had been taking place. Even in Tulum we had seen the streets patrolled by menacing looking police patrols, but in central Cancun these vehicles seemed to be everywhere. The matt black four by fours had an open back with a cradle surround. Three military police officers were in each. They were dressed head to foot in bullet proof armour, with some chunky articulated sections over their shoulders and knees. Under their matching matt black helmets they wore a balaclava and sun glasses. Their weapons were gripped tightly. Two held semi automatic rifles, whereas the third one had both hands on the trigger of a rear facing sub-machine gun.

Needless to say I survived a walk to and from a local restaurant, as well as the night, and a taxi ride back to the airport in the morning. The curse had lifted, and I took off on time.

Back in La Paz, Bolivia, I had twenty-four hours or so to tell everyone in my life what had happened. As well as upsetting my immediate family, I managed to upset Sue's immediately family too. They could not find it in their hearts to be happy for me. I was disappointed, saddened, and more than a little surprised by their initial reactions. In fact, over the next few months, a succession of vile emails arrived from both sides, castigating my character. On the other hand, without exception, every single one of my closest friends, as well as my new friends on social media, and those who had linked up with me to follow my journey, offered me warm congratulations. Hundreds of them got in touch to say so. Naturally I preferred the love and support that they offered, and decided again to postpone any attempt at recovering the love of the two families, until a later date. There was no point in trying at that moment.

18. Life in the high Andes.

The ride out of La Paz was simple enough. The bike had been safely looked after where I had left it in the hotel, and it was riding well. It took me to a high plain heading for the border with Peru. Back a to barren landscape and llamas again. Two weeks before hand, when I exited La Paz airport for Cancun, I was obliged to explain why there was no entry stamp in my passport. After paying a modest visitor fee, all was well. Customs officers at the Bolivia / Peru border post were now asking me the same questions about my bike. It took them quite a while to accept my explanation, eventually conceding: "There is no money in the east to patrol the border". Separately to my bike I had to pass through passport control and security. A tourist coach had just arrived to be processed before me. We were all in a brand new complex, with efficient uniformed staff. A senior officer seemed to be making sure the training regimes were being followed, and was almost marching up and down the ranks sternly observing the proceeding. The coach was full of young people who were on a grand tour of South America. A student from Denmark engaged me in interesting conversations. Just as I was beginning to make the entirely unreasonable assumption that this young crowd, mostly resembling the party-goers at an outdoor summer music festival in England, might be worth inspecting for drugs, the senior officer came to the same conclusion. He ordered a full airport-like scan and bag search for everybody, with sniffer dogs to assist. I shuffled forward, trying to remain patient, one person at a time. I was there for over two hours.

Three ladies sat at tables just beyond the new fence offered me a currency exchange service. They were all colourfully attired in traditional Peruvian costumes making it difficult for me to choose between them. I chose the one with the tallest hat, and was again surprised, as I was when entering Bolivia, by the generosity of her exchange rate.

A few minutes later I caught my first sight of Lake Titicaca. It looked chilly, clean and bountiful. The deep blue surface shimmered, and reflected the sun's rays back towards the azure sky. I could see fishing boats towards the horizon, and netted enclosures for aquaculture nearer the shore. The road on to Puno, my destination, was good quality and of some comfort to me. I settled in to a lakeside hotel, with llamas and dozens of guinea pigs in the garden, and organised a boat trip the following day. I was excited by the prospect of a visit out to the so-called floating islands. But first I had to find out why Lake Titicaca was known as the 'highest navigable lake in the world'. There were higher lakes and they have boats on them. Nestling in the port, looking a little rusty in places, was the SS Ollanta, birthed at 3,812 metres above sea level. It had only recently been taken out of service but for many years had operated a scheduled commercial service for goods and passengers between Bolivia and Peru. This was how they justified use of the word 'navigable'.

I decided that this was a self designated claim, but before I admonished it I reflected on my own claim. I had set out to become the first man in the world to ride the world's largest capacity production motorcycle around the world. All was factually correct. The Guinness Book of World Records had turned down my application for entry as they said my record was not a human achievement, and the record of being the 'first' to do something could not be beaten. They needed to publish new records every year. I accepted their decision, and was grateful for their reply. I acknowledged that my Triumph Rocket X was only currently the world's largest production motorcycle. One day there might be a larger one. Indeed, it was also Triumph's designation that the Rocket was the largest capacity production motorcycle in the world. Accurate, but self designated again. There were custom made bikes with larger engines, but they were never 'in production'. The 2,300 cc Triumph Rocket had been in continuous production for over ten years before I bought this one.

It was crisp, bright and dry as I slipped out of sight of the SS Ollanta with a dozen other tourists on a small boat, and out to visit the Uros tribe. No records existed but they are thought to have traveled to the shores of Lake Titicaca from Brazil, to create a farming and fishing life for themselves. Legend had it that to avoid attacks from other tribes already there, they sought sanctuary in the middle of the lake by constructing floating islands from the abundant giant reeds that line the shores; Tortora. Blocks of roots about the size of a bale of straw were cut then tied together to form a base about the size of a large house. Tortora reeds were then laid on top of the base. The result was dry to live on, and a little bouncy under foot. You can even eat the freshly cut end of a Tortora. It is soft, moist and fibrous, with a sweet taste. Add to that a diet of fish and ducks and the Uros tribe have managed to live like that for centuries. Tourism was now their major source of income, by far. We were shown inside a couple of their huts, made from dried Tortura. Very cosy. There was an offer to stay the night in one, but I declined. I left before the sun dipped and spent part of the evening reflecting on life as a Uros floating islander. They couldn't leave as I did. Their ancestors didn't leave at all. Life at 3,812 meters on a lake must have been very hard indeed.

Moving on, the next town looked like a forgotten outpost of a failed province, and clearly suffered from a lack of good town planning. Once past the lake, the road quality was adequate enough for me to be able to relax a little. There was stuff going on inside my helmet again which I needed to analyse. Thoughts were gathering and revolving, but without much of a conclusion. Something had changed inside me. I felt quite different and not only wondered why but also when this had started. The basics were plain enough. I had lost my first wife, the mother of our two sons, my best friend, as well as our company, and at least half my pension plan. I also had no income. Setting out to travel the world I was determined to rid myself of lingering prejudices, and was fairly confident that I had succeeded. I also had managed to convince myself that at my tender age I was not riding to 'discover' myself. Though I had learnt a great deal, devouring so many rich experiences, I was again confident that I was still the same man who had set out to offer himself to the world over a year ago. No, in fact I had changed. I must have done. This part of the changes I was feeling needed more work

for me to try and understand. The changes I was feeling on that day, high in the Andes, floating along from village to village, were not changes I had anticipated at the start. There was an inner contentment to me. If I had not earlier reached a conclusion about my religious beliefs, then I might have explained to myself that I was feeling holy inside. So that couldn't be it. I felt blissful and calm deep within. I felt wholly in accord with my world.
Bloody hell! I practically screeched to halt when I realised what had changed. It was obvious, but I hadn't had time to reflect upon it. I was married again.
That was the difference. I hadn't realised that was what had been missing. It wasn't just my love for Dalila, but was the fact that we were married. I knew there to be a snuggly, delicious, wholesome facet to marriage, and I knew I had lost that, but in that instant I realised it had come back. I was loving being married again. Dalila had sent me a photo of herself with a full glass of wine in her hand. Her expression had changed too, if only slightly, and I could see it reflected a change within her. There was a subtle air of contentment in her smile.

I was later to learn that after becoming a widower men typically saw their life as broken at that point, and sought to fix it. Without knowing that, I was happy to accept that I had been a typical widower in that respect. In fact, I thought this to be a gross simplification, but nevertheless acknowledged the principle to be probably true.

--- ---

One of the world's greatest mysteries is buried deep in this part of the Andes. An ancient, well organised, and successful culture, grew to dominate a vast kingdom. Rumours of hoards of gold drew invading conquistadors to their stronghold, the Inca capital of Cusco. However, it was probably smallpox, not the sword, that led to a swift end for a nearby citadel. Subsequently lost to the jungle for centuries, Machu Picchu had become the mysterious jewel that fascinated all, including myself.

It was re-discovered by American historian Hiram Bingham in 1911. Probably built about five hundred years before that, it had survived many earthquakes. Many other Peruvian buildings had turned to rubble in the meantime, but the foundations at Machu Picchu had been cut and worn to a smooth finish, and fitted neatly together. No mortar was used, or necessary, as the craftsmanship alone achieved a perfect result. Many stones were not square or rectangular but had multiple corners slotting together like a 3-D jigsaw. This prevented the walls from falling down. No one had been able to determine exactly how one particular stone with seventeen interlocking sides could have been so perfectly constructed.

With no written records in the Inca culture, historians were also still trying to establish exactly why Machu Picchu was built, how it was used and why it was abandoned. It would appear that the majority of inhabitants, approximately one thousand, were women and children, together with a few male priests. Skeletal records have led some to think that the citadel existed to protect children and help insure future generations. Others think that there must have been fighting men there too, but that they did not return from battle. Even so, there was no evidence that Spanish conquistadors found Machu Picchu. The Spanish found Cusco, about eighty kilometres up the Urubamba river, destroyed much of it, and re-built it in their style. The historic centre was truly reminiscent of that period. Ollantaytambo, Sacsayhuaman, Pisac and Moray, all near to Cusco, were well worth a visit.

I found the llamas at Machu Picchu to be more inquisitive than their gormless cousins in Patagonia. Perhaps only those with the highest intelligence, and the best exam results, were chosen to guide tourists in the Inca citadel. At every other opportunity we were able to take home a llama with us. Made from wool, wood, metal, china, glass, plastic and paper, in every conceivable size, tourists were never short of a chance to purchase one on a whim either in Cusco or Aguas Calientes, the town directly below Machu Picchu.

— — —

My little ride around South America to this point, enabled me to tick a list. I had now visited all of the New Seven Wonders of the World in my lifetime; five on this trip.

After researching, I learnt that the list was not necessarily as definitive as I had previously thought. In fact, it was controversial. The only survivor from the Ancient Seven Wonders of the World list, compiled over 2000 years before, was the Great Pyramid. Egyptian authorities objected to its inclusion in a vote. It was subsequently withdrawn and given "Honorary Wonder" status. So, the list of seven was now to be a list of eight.

The vote was the brainchild of a Swiss marketing organisation who claimed it to be a 'not for profit' operation. However, it was clear that a good deal of money changed hands, as countries competed with each other to be included.

The organisation claimed that this was the largest poll in history with over 100 millions votes cast.

Several countries had celebrities, media and government departments engaged to energise people to vote. Via the internet, each person was only allowed one vote. However, by telephone, there was no restriction on the number of times people could vote. Telephone companies in Rio de Janeiro, for example, not only allowed the phone call to made free of charge, but sent texts to their customers advising them that they could 'vote now for free'.

The new list was not recognised by United Nations Educational, Scientific and Cultural Organization (UNESCO) who made it clear that all sites on their World Heritage List have equal importance.

Here's the list, and with my opinion of each:
1. Taj Mahal, India.
The most exquisite building I had ever seen. Emotions tugged in every direction. The setting, design, craftsmanship, materials and purpose were all perfect. Built for love.
2. Machu Picchu, Peru.

The remote Inca citadel, lost to the jungle for centuries, fascinated me for its location, construction, purpose and atmosphere. Magical.

3. Petra, Jordan.

The Nabatean 'Rose City' trading hub featured rock-cut architecture, water conduit systems, and a long entrance gorge called the Siq. All remarkable.

4. The Colosseum, Rome, Italy.

The iconic Roman 'sports' stadium and entertainment complex impressed me by its scale as well as gladiatorial atmosphere.

5. Great Wall of China, China.

The largest structure on the list, and famously visible from space. It was a very big wall.

6. Christ the Redeemer, Rio de Janeiro, Brazil.

The youngest on the list was already a cultural icon, looking down on Rio with a slightly bowed head and arms outstretched. Beguiling.

7. Chichen Itza, Yucatan, Mexico.

At the centre of the Mayan city, the Castillo temple demonstrated their understanding of astronomy. Not so remarkable.

8. Great Pyramid of Giza, Egypt.

Immense pyramid from around 2560BC. It was the world's largest man-made structure for over 3,800 years. Wow!

If I had my way I would put the Great Pyramid in at number two, and bump Chichen Itza off the list.

I would also add Angkor Wat, Cambodia, and lose Christ the Redeemer. But as I didn't vote, I can't do that.

— — —

I was never quite sure why, but none of the hotels I stayed in Peru had central heating systems. Perhaps it was down to cost. At 3,400 metres above sea level, Cusco was chilly at night, and I was only given a small electric heater for company when confined to bed for thirty-six hours with an upset stomach, the first and only illness of my entire journey.

The technically challenging ride out of Cusco, via wet cobbled streets with tight switchbacks, was all the more difficult with a delicate stomach, but eased as I reached open countryside. The high Andes started to reward me with some glorious scenery. Rarely flat, I ascended and descended throughout most of the day, stopping frequently to admire the views. Deep green valleys contrasted with lighter greens over the hills. Anywhere just about flat enough for cultivation or animal husbandry was in use.

Around one particular corner a man with a flag waved me down. A landslide had blocked half of the road ahead. In fact, it looked liked half a mountain had been rolling downhill for several days, across the road, and then down the other side. Most of the material was useful quarry sized pieces, but larger boulders were tumbling with them. Everybody wanting to progress their day had a judgement to make. One vehicle from my side, then one vehicle from the other side, waited, observed, then gambled that a thirty second window would be safe enough for them to get to through. Only one car picked up a small dent, but I was lucky. When I reached the far side I pulled over to speak to a friend. In fact there was no-one there that I knew, but whilst waiting I recalled a story that an Italian restaurant manager in Cork, Ireland, had told me on the first week of my journey. He had worked for a few years in South America and had met fellow bikers during his time there. A little like me he had taken off on a two wheeled adventure in Peru, and had also encountered a landslide in the Andes. His was larger than mine, and halted his progress for several days. When eventually cleared he emerged the other side and was dismayed to find a Brazilian friend he had once worked with, waiting to make his way through on a bike in the opposite direction.

During the following day the landscape started to lose its colour. It became arid, and adobe mud bricks emerged as a popular choice for building construction on the higher planes and passes. I started to descend towards the Pacific coast as the dusty hillsides gave way to desert-like undulations. They had worn to a largely flat, grey, landscape as I neared Nascar.

In Erich von Däniken's book 'Chariots of the Gods' he claimed that the Nazca Lines were some sort of instruction from extraterrestrial beings - airfields for their spaceships. I couldn't understand why more scientists had not lambasted him for the suggestion. I am not a scientist, but I thought his suggestion was ludicrous, though his skills as an author and book salesman were considerable.

The lines in the Nazca desert in south Peru, were created by indigenous populations between 500BC and 500AD. They were created for cultural and religious purposes, mostly messages to their gods. There were many straight lines, and the shapes of about seventy animals, trees and flowers. The animals included huge outlines of a monkey, hummingbird and fish. Scooping the reddish-brown top soil away left their work to be clearly seen in the limestone rock below. They don't have to be viewed from space. The hills nearby allowed most to be seen easily enough, or the scaffold tower that I climbed. I saw a 'tree', albeit upside-down.

19. Lost in Lima.

Thinking of my journey ahead, as always, I sent off an online application for a USA visa waiver, using their ESTA system. I had done the same many times before in ... ... as I was a regular visitor. The questions were as simple as they used to be but an extra tick-box had been added. It asked me if I had visited any one of six countries in recent years, including Iran. Of course I had to tick the box. The usual email reply did not arrive as promptly as I had expected, so I had to return to the site and fish for one. "Not authorised for travel" was the message I found, in bold.

There was no explanation given, but further down the page I learnt that I could apply for a full visa. This was as far as I had got when I learnt at Cancun airport that I could not even transit through Miami without one or the other.

Before arriving in Lima I had applied for the full visa. The application form asked many more questions but as I had nothing to hide I was happy to answer them. The process included wanting to know my full travel history for the previous five years, and would be concluded by a face to face interview at a US Consulate of my choosing. There was one in Lima.

Two days after arriving I duly followed a very regimental set of instructions to arrive, on time of course, for my interview. There was at least two hundred people already there for visa processing when I arrived, and I think I was the only gringo. My interview turned out to be a shouting match through a bullet-proof glass window. I answered a couple of questions but was denied an opportunity to offer more information about my journey. The officer spoke to a colleague and returned to tell me that more questions would be sent to me by e-mail from the State Department in Washington, USA. He would not confirm that my ride through Iran the previous year was the concern, and when I pushed him he didn't give me a straight answer. I left only assuming it was.

The extra questions from the State Department arrived within seven days as he said they would. I replied within twenty-four hours, this time detailing my full travel history for the previous fifteen years. I even gave them my last passport number so they could check my US entry and exit history. The form also allowed me to offer more information. I made it clear that I had been nothing but a friend of America for most of my adult life. I had visited at least thirty times, for business as well as for vacations, and was proud to boast that included travelling to thirty-nine states to that point. I was hoping to complete the fifty with my next visit. I also pointed out that, in the good years, my company had bought about a million dollars worth of US made goods every year.

Iranian citizens, amongst others, had been banned from entering the US at this point. There was no ban in place for UK citizens who had merely visited Iran as a tourist.

There was nothing, I considered, to give the decision maker any concern about me. The waiting process started on the eighth day.

I didn't take the earthquake that struck Lima a few days later as a bad omen, but perhaps I should have done. It was quite a serious one, and woke me at six in the morning with my room shaking, quite violently for a few seconds. Measured at 5.2 on the Richter scale, it was common enough in the central Andes region. There was no damage, and no reports of any injuries.

— — —

Meanwhile I checked my bike in to Triumph Lima for an oil change and new tyres. The last set had not worn out yet, but as I was heading north through Central America I wanted to feel confident that a fresh set of rubber might give me the best chance of avoiding a puncture. Triumph had dealers in most countries on my planned route, but the next tyre change would likely be in the USA. I was not too pleased to discover that although Rockets had been sold in Peru, the tyres were not stocked. After searching for a way forward I was left with no option but to accept an expensive solution. I had to get them imported from Miami. The city that would not let me in, but would let my tyres out!

Waiting for both the service and the visa, I was lucky enough to be able to catch up with friends, passing through. Quite by chance I had spotted an article in Traverse magazine by Suzie Bostock. I was surprised to learn that she and partner Kelvin had grabbed time out to enjoy a motorcycle adventure around South America, taking at least a year to do so. Their bikes were perfect for off road experiences, making their adventure quite different to mine. I had known Suzie all her life, as well as her brother Ben who had recently visited them in Cusco. I caught up with them in Lima, and learnt all about their travels. Talking so enthusiastically about experiencing the start of the Dakar Rally left me more than a little envious.

A further glorious surprise was to follow. I had met Stephen and Alexandra at Uluru, central Australia. They were beside me at sunset. Their round-the-world tour, in stages but not on two wheels, had got them as far as Lima. Having celebrated my last birthday on my own in Istanbul the previous year, I intended to take full advantage of them being here for my next birthday. I booked us in to one the best restaurants in Lima, and together we managed to get through fifteen courses, each quite small though, over a very lazy four hour lunch. It was truly a magnificent meal, and not at all expensive by European standards. A few years beforehand Peru had realised that the size and shape of the country offered huge bio-diversity, and started to develop a food culture to promote that to the world.

— — —

My days were spent mostly walking around the Miraflores district where I was staying. Ever increasing circles kept me fit enough, and boosted my confidence about being in Lima. I paced up and down the high cliff path running along the coast too. From there, paragliders took off seawards, then swung confidently to run parallel to the cliff edge, occasionally skipping over trees and buildings, before returning to descend over everyone's head. Ice cream vendors caught my attention most days, and at weekends all the headland park areas were full of picnickers and cyclists. The shortest strolls were in the mid morning to a favourite coffee shop. A lunchtime regular was deliciously fresh bagels with cream cheese and avocado, washed down with fresh homemade lemonade. I settled on a choice of five simple restaurants for the evenings. One was run by an Englishman, another was Indian, a further was typical Peruvian, and two more were Italian. I felt comfortable in all of them, though not many enabled me to talk to locals. English was not widely spoken. However, in one of the Italian restaurants, whilst waiting for the bill to be delivered, I suffered from my new found confidence in humanity, and Lima residents in particular. The restaurant was not busy. A beggar slipped in and took a direct line towards me. I turned my head away, trying to avoid eye contact, and shook it. He offered me a piece of paper to read, possibly indicating he was mute or deaf. I turned away again, but he moved closer with the paper, then swiftly disappeared. Only a few seconds later I realised he had taken my iPhone, hidden from my view by his piece of paper. I ran up and down the street but he had already disappeared. The Police were called and I was taken to the station for a form filling exercise. All a waste of time of course. The phone had gone, the SIM card removed, and possibly sold on within minutes. Petty theft is common in Lima, but that was of little consolation to me. In the morning I spent a few hours finding a replacement in a multi-story electrical goods warehouse, full of used phones, perhaps some stolen from tourists. For a while I thought I might even come across mine again. I didn't. My Plan A to cope with a loss like this was always to just buy another. iCloud saved the day, and I moved on.

— — —

Of some comfort to me, considerably so to be honest, was the fact that the FIFA World Cup was on whilst I was there. Peruvians love their football, and so do I. Peru kicked off their preparations by hosting a friendly game against Scotland and for a few days the Miraflores district was home to several hundred Scotland supporters, mostly sporting magnificent kilts, sporrans, garters and caps with feathers, finished off with a Scotland football shirt. Six of them stayed in my hotel and were good company.

Over the weeks I managed to watch every single game; a feat never achieved by me in any previous finals. I thoroughly enjoyed it, watching some of the games, or at least some of the halves, in locals bars and cafes. Most were watched alone in my room, where I was easily able to construct my days around the published schedules. The quality of play was excellent, though some games were more entertaining than others. England progressed well, better than expected, and France too. Both reached the semi-final stage and I was forced to consider the dilemma of them in the final against each other. How would I handle the country I had of course supported all my life, but left, against the country where I had now chosen to live? The dilemma was resolved for me by England's elimination at the hands of Croatia, and left me able to go crazy with my new French family and friends, shouting *"Allez les Bleus"* until the final whistle, and beyond.

— — —

I woke every day hoping that an email would arrive from the US Consulate to tell me my visa application had been approved. Every day I was disappointed. Every day I lay on my hotel bed staring at the four walls and ceiling. Every day my sanity slipped away a little. Every day I tried to regain it and stay positive. Every day became more difficult.

The visa application clearly stated that the process could take up to sixty days to complete. I didn't want to believe that could possibly be the case for me. It also clearly stated that I could not contact them in the meantime. However, I ignored that and sent one email every week. Someone unaffectionately called 'Consular Section' sent me a reply every time. Variously it would state "the process cannot be expedited", or "you will be contacted when the process is complete", or "we advise you not to confirm travel arrangements in advance". There was never a direct response to the contents of my emails to them. I pointed out that I was passing through Lima on an around-the-world journey. I pointed out that I simply had nothing to do except wait for them to process my application. I pointed out that I was staring at four walls and a ceiling, going steadily more crazy one day at a time. I tried pleading, in a pathetic 'please help me I'm a British citizen' manner. I tried a little humour too. I even tried being politely grumpy. Nothing worked. If I was a Peruvian, one of the two hundred being processed daily, then I could get on with my life whilst waiting for the application process to be concluded. I told them that was not the case. I couldn't understand where the problem might be. As my emails surely reminded them that I was still waiting, I felt reasonably certain that I had not been filed away and forgotten about. If Washington had done their job then they would not have found anything about me that they wouldn't like. I had paid for the visa application service so expected a service in return.

I also pointed out that they had let in two acquaintances of mine after they had ridden through Iran. One had a current visa waiver before riding through Iran. Another had a full visa processed in London before he left. Both arrived at the US border and received an unpleasant and lengthy interview, but both were allowed in. So why not me?

I even visited the British Consulate in Lima to ask for their help. I thought that they might be able to phone a friend in the US Consulate and draw their attention to my application. I had a reference number of course. They declined to help me, but were polite about it.

Dalila was immeasurably helpful, constantly suggesting different tactics, and motivating me every day with her support and love.

She also encouraged me to deal with my family problems at home, rebuilding broken bridges. A tiny issue was resolved by the discovery of an on-line postcard service. The App allowed me to download a photo of where I had been, write a few carefully chosen words, add a UK address, pay a remarkably small fee, and have the UK arm print and post it for me. I sent several to my mother who loved to receive them. The world of postcard sending from holiday destinations was in decline. Often, wherever I was able to buy them, the vendor was not able to sell me a stamp or offer to post them for me. On my journey to this point I had not been able to send her very many. Whilst stuck in Lima I at least also had the time to work out where to buy writing paper and envelopes, as well as to figure out how the postal system to the UK worked. I sent my mother a lengthy hand written letter, trying to explain the need for my journey to her, articulating not only what had happened but also why it had happened. I also phoned her several times, recognising that my communications had been poor. I was travelling with eleven different communication tools at my disposal, but pushed the telephone to the bottom of the list as it was the most expensive to use, and least convenient for me as I was always in a different time zone to everyone else. My mother was very much the matriarch of the whole family, and the most important for me to offer an olive branch. I never lost her love, but sensed that I had challenged it.

― ― ―

If only I had known at the outset that the visa application process would take so long, I could have made a decision or two to explore Peru further. Waiting there every day for news was what had kept me in Lima. I took a risk and booked a four day exit. At least I thought, with luck running against me, I might hear the day after I reserved the trip, that my visa had been granted. It wasn't.

I flew out early one morning for a flight to the extreme north east of Peru at Iquitos. The mighty Amazon river starts further to the south but by the time it reached Iquitos it was already two kilometres wide. It was 3,600 kilometres from its mouth but huge ocean going ships could steam up the river to this point and load with oil and timber for export.
Noise, belching traffic, excessive use of their horns, a busy commercial centre and imperfect infrastructure all reminded me that I was still in Peru. The heat, humidity, jungle and fast flowing river arrived like a slap in the face, and woke me up to a different world. Suddenly I felt I wasn't in Peru at all, but isolated from civilisation and its political borders. My lodge, up a tributary called Rio Momon, was an entirely wooden complex, built on stilts, regularly suffering from flooding, but entirely in keeping with my anticipated jungle adventure. The sounds, from

birds mainly, completed the picture and sent me in to a kind of sensory overload.

Within an hour I had a sloth clinging to me. Its long fury arms were around my neck, as I cuddled and cradled it like a baby. It moved in slow motion from left to right and then stretched out to one side to grasp a nearby branch. A younger sloth was not quite so keen to play. Neither was the adult Anaconda that my guide slipped over my shoulders a few moments later. It slithered and wriggled and didn't feel cuddly at all. There was quite a range of exotics in this caged jungle clearing, including some gorgeous looking scarlet macaws, as well a tapir with an absurdly sized erect penis.

After a good meal and restful night I woke to a dawn chorus from wild turkeys and cockerels outside my door. First on the agenda was a fishing trip in a wooden canoe. A hook on a fixed line was all we needed to ensure success. I caught a Piranha, and that thrilled me beyond reason. It was later prepared for my lunch - very tasty but just fishy. Its teeth were admirable.

Another boat took me deeper up the tributary, and a path led to a tribal village in a clearing. I was encouraged to try my hand at using a blow pipe. A dart with feather was inserted at the mouth end, and once I had stopped waving the open end about too much, a short blow was all it needed to send it to a target high up a post, scoring a hit. I was shown hand made gifts to buy, of remarkable quality in fact, and had a group of ladies sing a chant. All a bit too touristy for me at that moment I thought, but I'm unlikely to experience the same again.

My guide and I had got on quite well by this point so he didn't hesitate to take me deeper in to the jungle, this time with a machete in hand. He explained that tourists from Asia and North America rarely handled jungle trekking well, but Europeans and Australians coped better. I couldn't let the side down, so I ventured on beside him with confidence. My light summer footwear proved quite inadequate for what was to follow. Mud and streams mostly. I slithered along and only just managed to keep up. One of the stream crossing points had no more than a flattened tree trunk for us to use, with sticks in the river bed for me to grab for balance. In due course we reached a magnificent old Lupuna tree, revered by the local tribe. On the way back he took me down a side track to a clearing with Coca trees under cultivation. He then revealed to me the importance of cocaine production to the local sub-economy, with scarcely a blink as he did so.

Butterflies and pigmy marmosets were a highlight on the last day, as well as a stroll around Iquitos centre where I admired a metal house, built during the late nineteenth century rubber boom period, allegedly designed by French architect Gustave Eiffel.

The slap in the face on arrival had to be matched by a slap on the other cheek when I left. I had to wake myself up to the fact that I really had experienced an incredible adventure on the Amazon, a world away from my life in Europe, crammed in to just a few days.

———

Before arriving in Peru I had a good idea where the rest of my journey would take me. The immediate route was obvious, and would be through Ecuador to Colombia. From there I would hop over the Darien Gap, on through Central America, then Mexico, and then in to USA. Whilst in the States I would ride a bit of a convoluted route to cover the nine more contiguous States that I had never previously visited. On through Canada to Alaska would get me to my forty-ninth State, then a flight to Hawaii for a long weekend would enable me to proudly boast that I had visited all fifty States in my lifetime.

Various forces were now gathering to prevent all of my goals being achieved. The Canada, Alaska and Hawaii idea would take more time and money than I thought would be prudent to commit, after all. I could complete a round-the-world journey by heading directly from Mexico to a grand New York finish without anybody suggesting I had cut a corner. I could get back to Dalila and my new life in Lyon sooner rather than later.

There was also a growing problem in Nicaragua. Students and retirees had been in the streets to protest about government changes to their financial position. They had been met by bullets, and hundreds had been reported dead. The rest of the country joined in, and had blocked all the major roads. I was keeping an eye on the news, and reports by adventurers passing through, both on four wheels and two. Travellers were being stopped but not really threatened. Instead they were being escorted around the road blocks, and over fields. Not my Rocket's favourite route. However, I decided to give it a go. Getting around the Darien Gap - the border region of southern Panama where no roads have been built because of the terrain - was also of some concern. I intended to take a boat from the northern Colombian port of Cartagena to Colon in Panama at the mouth of the canal. There was a ferry service for a while, but that had shut down. I could have the bike crated and fed in to a container again, and suffer all the inconvenience and expense of port procedures once more, this time in tropical heat, with an under current of anti-narcotics trafficking obstacles to add to the mix. It too was doable.

All of this depended on the visa application still being processed by the US Consulate in Lima.

I set to work on a Plan B. Certainly I could ride to Colombia. I could pay to get around the Garien gap. I could risk the roads in Nicaragua. I could ride on to the Mexico / USA border. Then I would have to stop and wait again, possibly with a fresh visa application submitted to the US Consulate in Mexico City. I wasn't confident that would be a better process than in Lima.

Plan C was to fly over USA to Canada and have my grand finish in Montreal or Toronto. I contacted three Mexico to Canada air cargo companies I found on-line, as well as Triumph and Harley in Mexico, and sent yet another cry for help to Motofreight in London. They had put me in contact with known motorcycle freight companies in Dubai and Delhi earlier in my journey. None of them could help me. There simply was no service available to fly one motorcycle out of Mexico into Canada. I could send a dozen bikes in a shipping container, but I neither had a dozen nor could afford to wait another thirty days or probably more for yet another sea passage.

Plan D, it emerged, was to crate the bike in Bogota, Colombia, and have it flown to Vancouver, Canada. I didn't like Plan D. It felt like giving up. I would miss out all of the Central American cultures I had been so looking forward to experiencing. I would not be crossing, or even seeing, the Panama Canal. Much like

The Taj Mahal, Mount Everest, and Uluru, seeing the Panama Canal one day had been a dream since my early school days. Worst of all, I would miss all of my friends in the US. I had wanted to visit them in Texas, California, Oregon, Colorado, Ohio, Georgia, New Jersey and New York.

I never devised a Plan E. I was sick of trying to solve this problem. What was wrong with me? Why didn't the USA like me anymore? I was still the man I was before riding through Iran. I fully respected every country's right to protect its border as it saw fit. I had crossed enough borders in the previous year to prove that, and confirm my respect. I was content in principle to go through the US evaluation process, but could not accept their failure to respond to me. I was getting close to the fiftieth day waiting for a reply, and decided to act on Plan D then. One more email to chase the US Consulate led to one more reply. This time the "can take up to sixty days" reply changed to "can take several months".

Plan D had be enacted, and I decided to leave Lima without a US visa.

— — —

Just before doing so, two important pieces of administration had to be completed.

The first was to send my Carnet de Passage en Douane back to the UK for discharge. Carnets are only valid for a year and mine had just a couple of weeks left to run. I had been able to determine with reasonable certainty that none of the countries ahead of me on my route would need to use my Carnet. Every page had both an entry stamp and an exit stamp as instructed. Once safely received and verified, my cash deposit could be returned to me.

Not as valuable in itself, but certainly more important, was our Mexican *'Acta de Matrimonio'* certificate. Dalila had returned to Lyon and rushed round to the Town Hall only to be told there were several steps ahead for us before France would accept this as a genuine certificate. In other words, we were not yet married in the eyes of French law. This was a bitterly disappointing blow to both of us, but she set about correcting it. As well as the usual paperwork, such as proof of address, utility bills, copy of birth certificate and so on, she was also being asked for an Apostille to be applied to the original marriage certificate. Neither of us had any idea what that was, let alone how to go about getting it. We learnt that the Apostille Convention of 1961 legalises and allows a document certified in one member country to be accepted in all member countries. Mexico and France were signatories to the Convention, and a Marriage Certificate qualified as a legal document. So, our Marriage Certificate had to go back to Mexico.

When she sent it to me shortly after I arrived in Lima, the idea was that I would ride with it through Mexico on my way to the USA. In the meantime I needed to find out who could apply the Apostille, effectively a second rubber stamp and signature next to the original rubber stamp and signature that our Judge had applied on our wedding day. We were slipping further away from that lovely romantic idea of marrying in Mexico. The *'Registro Civil'* in Tulum could not help us, but I chanced upon a Notary there who could. They in turn would take in to an administration office in Chetumal, six hours south of Tulum on the Mexico / Belize border, return seven days later to collect it, with the Apostille stamp applied, and return it to Lyon. His fee was quite reasonable for all that.

As I had just decided not to ride through Mexico after all, but jump over it, both document packages were sent off using an International courier service, and all fingers were tightly crossed.

In addition, Dalila also had to get the certificate translated into French, using a French government approved translation service.

20. Fertility bottoms.

It was good to be back on the bike again, although the north Lima suburbs seemed to drag on forever. Thanks to Kelvin and Suzie I was able to spot and carefully ride around the glass that was strewn over the carriageway in several places, just before a number of puncture repair businesses.

The landscape quickly reverted to the near desert-like grey environment that dominated my ride in from the south, and was no more interesting despite being imaginatively named the "Trans American Highway".

The road to Ecuador lead me inland slightly, and slowly but surely I gained altitude towards the Andes once more.

The border posts out of Peru and in to Ecuador had almost no traffic passing through and processed me efficiently.

Entering Ecuador I immediately noticed that large tracts of fertile land had been maximised for their potential. I rode for at least a hundred and sixty kilometres with nothing but banana plantations on either side of the road. It was a huge cash crop for the country, and a staple for companies like Chiquita, Dole and Del Monte. I was slightly concerned though by the numerous light aircraft spraying insecticides, not only over the banana trees, but also over the road that I was riding.

Further on it was pineapples, passion fruit, papaya and other exotic fruits most evidently under cultivation, as well as processing and canning plants.

Sugar cane dominated the landscape for a while, all carted away in huge articulated containers longer than the 'road trains' of the Australian bush.

I crossed the Equator just north of Ecuador's capital, Quito. The Quitsato Sundial is the highest point on the Equator in the world. The shadow created by its design apparently showed solstices and equinoxes with accuracy, but I couldn't hang around to see for myself. As my bike was at sea when it passed over the Equator heading south near Indonesia, I was pleased to have had this opportunity to stop and reflect again on my journey. I sat and contemplated for a few minutes, with one foot either side of the painted line. My left foot was in the Southern Hemisphere, and my right was closer to home in the Northern. Wondering how I managed to get to this point, not just in the physical sense, I couldn't help feeling pleased with myself. I had just seen a purpose-built overland truck in the car park run by a company I had met in London. An idea I had when talking to them over a year ago was to follow the bus on my bike throughout South America. At the time I was looking for a suitable but interesting route and thought the idea of riding with them would also help me feel a little more secure. In fact, at the adventure travel exhibition where I had met them, the idea lasted for no more than a couple of minutes. It was just a conversation. But here I was, high in Ecuador, straddling the Equator, almost five months after arriving in South America, thoroughly enjoying my solo adventure. I didn't need them after all.

I gave out an audible, satisfied sigh, stepped over the line, and rode on.

The riding was easy in Ecuador, and the simple hotels were good for the price. Crossing out of the country in to Colombia could hardly have been more different than entering. Thousands of people were crammed in to every building, on to every pavement, and across almost every road. Barriers were ignored, as too were shouts from officials. The Police and Army were overwhelmed by it all, and so was I. Feeding my way on the bike to where a couple of other bikes had pulled up attracted more attention than I thought comfortable. These were not the usual admiring glances, but were piercing stares of envy. Every single one of these people seemed to have less than me, and looked desperate. They wore multiple layers of clothing despite the midday heat. Much of that looked dirty. Many of the adults were sat or lying on plastic bags of clothing, and many of the children were sat on the adults. Some had food; just rice, bread, fruit and pulses. Something had gone wrong with their lives, but I didn't find out what that was until later.

I stepped over a few bodies to reach the end of the Ecuador passport control, and shuffled forward solemnly. Tempers were running high in the chaotic cacophony and heat. A woman fainted but no one came to her aid, at first. A few hours passed slowly, but eventually I emerged with my passport stamped, and headed for the Colombia side. There was a line for passports, another for registering the bike, and a third one for buying road insurance. Lengthy processes, but calmer. By the time I got through I decided to venture no further than the border town for the night. I asked some locals, having a beer and watching some football on a television, why there were so many people waiting at the border. Apparently they were all from Venezuela, fleeing from rampant crime, political violence, hyper-inflation, and empty food shelves. I had been in the middle one of the largest mass-migrations in South American history with about three to four thousand people passing through each day. Their goal was to get to Ecuador, Peru or Chile where others before them had sought sanctuary.

— — —

Before the awful civil war broke out in Syria in 2011, I travelled through both Syria and Lebanon. It was a fabulous trip, full of discovery about the ancient civilisation and culture in the region, led by a well trained Syrian guide. He spoke good English. Heading westwards, we travelled over Lebanon's eastern mountain range, past the ancient cedar forests, and into the Bekaa Valley. The vegetation changed sharply, with arid hillsides giving way to the lush flat valley below. Our guide described the scene as a "fertility bottom". We resisted a snigger as we all knew what he meant. From that moment onwards, every fertile valley floor had been a fertility bottom to me. There were many in the Andes of Ecuador and Colombia, and they all appeared as important for sustaining local populations as any I had seen. They varied in size. Some were little more than a plot with vegetables and a goat. Larger ones had a variety of vegetables and fruit, and several goats. Some had terraces, and some were naturally flat valley floors. Others were mature, well cultivated, and commercialised. They not only sustained local populations, but provided employment and profit. However, they were all still fertility bottoms to me.

— — —

I was disappointed in Colombia, not because of the country itself, but because I had decided to head directly to Bogota and fly out of it. I would miss the northern half, and not even experience the beautiful looking port of Cartagena. My route hurried me towards the capital rather than allowing me to take a more convoluted, relaxed ride. Impatiently, I ignored the potential rewards of the country. The landscape was stunning. Many riding before me had tried to describe it, some even stating that it was their favourite country on their around-the-world journey, but even so, my expectations were exceeded. After two days I was still in the high Andes, cornering cautiously to gasp at so many beautiful vistas beyond.

On the higher ground, the coffee bean was king. Bushes clung to steep hillsides, with others on shallow terraces. Once picked, the coffee berry was often left to be dried in flat concrete areas beside the road, or even in the unused centre of roads, giving off a rotting fruit smell as it did so. Riding past Cali and towards to Medellín led me to reflect once more on cocaine production and the drug cartels who were based here in the past. I realised that coffee could not be as valuable a crop, but learnt that some people, perhaps quite a few, had been educated and supported to switch production. At least the FARC guerrillas had given up their guns after fifty years of fighting. A new peace and reconciliation process was helping next generation Colombians deal with the past, as explained to me by a small group in my Popayán hotel who were there working to that end.

The final half-day ride in to Bogotá, my last moments on the road in the Andes, reminded me of it's fragility. A substantial landslide had blocked and partially destroyed the arterial road over a high pass, thankfully this time, a few hours after I had passed through. The evening news headlines explained that the road would likely be shut for several weeks. Fatigued, late and lost, I crawled in to a hotel, relieved but greatly saddened that my South American adventure was over.

The friendly hoteliers took me just a few doors down the street to the equally friendly shipping company; Cargo Rider. In fact they offered me the best option for flying a bike from Bogotá to Panama, should I ever find myself riding their way again. They arranged for the Rocket to be cleaned and crated once more, before being presented to Customs. The final process took 24 hours to complete, with some officious security and anti-narcotics dogs giving the bike, and myself, a very thorough sniff, before loading.

21. Trump(ed)

I arrived in Vancouver, Canada a day ahead of my bike. Just one day waiting was a good deal shorter than the lengthy waits of the past, but it still wasn't a good day. My ....warded patience with the USA visa application process in Peru had transitioned from a period of disappointment, to anger. I had emailed the US Consulate in Vancouver to explain my situation, and asked if I could start a fresh application with them. I told them I hoped they would extend the courtesy of an expedited process this time. The reply to my email, promptly received, was encouraging at first. However, the on-line visa application form itself had frustrated me in Lima, and again in Vancouver. It seemed to have been written in a by-gone era, full of dis-functions, and frequently crashing on me. An associated website, but not the same one, told me how much the application fee would be, but not how to pay it. It also told me that if the application was successful, the Consulate would courier my stamped passport to a Canada Post office of my choice, where it would be handed to me on presentation of a Canada ID card and proof of address. Emailing the person at the Consulate to resolve both payment and collection problems for me, led to an increasingly frustrating series of replies in which I was redirected each time to the on-line pages which I had already explained contained the problems that I sought to resolve. My final email to them involved bold print and the phrase "utterly useless".

At some point in my life I hoped to be let back in to the USA again, but, at that moment, I concluded that there was only one person to blame for their ineptitude, failure of process, and current parochial attitude: President Trump.

In early 2017 he signed an Executive Order titled 'Protecting the Nation from Foreign Terrorist Entry into the United States'. It was widely known as a ban on Muslims for a while, but in fact stated that Nationals from the following countries were to be banned from entry: Iran, Iraq, Libya, Yemen, Syria, Somalia, Sudan, and North Korea. The ban was challenged by the courts of several States, and amended slightly later. However, on 26th.

June 2018 the Supreme Court upheld the President's authority to make the Order. A decision taken right in the middle of my waiting period in Lima. Although it generally placed limits on travel to the US, it was clearly directed at Nationals from those countries. I was not an Iranian National. I had never lived there and had not tried to travel directly from there to the US. I was a U.K citizen, escorted by a government registered guide on my once in a lifetime nine day ride through the country. How could that make me a threat to the US? That's what made me angry.

I wasn't terribly happy being in Vancouver either. Hotels seemed unreasonably expensive after South America, and I found the tipping culture in cafes and restaurants difficult to accept. With all my past experiences of North America, I should have been better prepared for both. I also disliked the fact that sales taxes were not displayed on products, but were added at the cash register. A deception that I found myself wanting to tell shopkeepers was not acceptable in my country.
On a different note entirely, I was staggered to see drug addicts injecting themselves in the recessed doorway of an empty shop next to my hotel. This was not a clandestine activity, but was happening in full daylight as tourists, shoppers and children walked by. The City of Vancouver offered overdose and prevention support to addicts from a building nearby, and in doing so had attracted more sufferers to the area. A laudable enough idea I suppose given a high drug related mortality rate in British Columbia, but although I acknowledge it would not be popular next to anyone's home, I couldn't help feeling that the commercial and tourist centre of the city might not be the best place.

On a sunny Sunday in July, a lengthy walk around Stanley Park was more than enough to brighten anyone's mood, mine included. Modern day artwork installations forced a smile, and a cluster of Totem poles fascinated and entertained me superbly. The footpath clung to the edge of Vancouver Harbour before revealing an inlet and the ocean beyond. A symphony orchestra played a waltz at Sunset Beach Park and had me feigning gentle circles in my head as I floated passed the bandstand.

The following day completed my welcome to Canada, with the simplest, shortest, least expensive airport and customs procedure of my entire journey. It took scarcely an hour before I rode away, without receiving a demand to pay for disposal of my crate, and without any of the past issues regarding tyre pressure, fuel, or battery connection.

My final destination was in the extreme east, but I couldn't go in that direction without seeing something of the Canadian Rockies first. They were north of Vancouver.

Almost immediately out of the city the road started twisting. And rising too, slowly. I caught glimpses of the sea and Vancouver Island over my left handlebar, then the promise of mountains over my right. Before I knew it though, I had left the Pacific coast for good. Light wispy clouds lay like locks of hair in a pool of bright blue sky. Peaks still with a little snow on them shaped my horizon, and carpets of thick natural forests and wild meadows ran downhill to my road. This was gorgeous country, and filled my heart. The towns of Squamish and Whistler were known to me by name, but I rode through and beyond them. A simple looking ranch with cabins looked appealing to stop for a bite to eat. Two other bikers pulled up after me and a conversation soon followed over a decent burger and fries. When questioned, I explained my journey to them. For the first time since I left Australia, our common language allowed us to explain our lives to each other with ease. One of them, only a little younger than me, was a widower, and the other, his brother in law. Tom had ridden with his late wife in the past and had planned to enjoy several more adventures together on two wheels, once money and children permitted. They never got to that point. I suggested venturing alone to him, but despite the intervening few years, he explained that he wasn't ready to do that yet. It served to remind me that everybody handled grief differently, and some people needed more time than others. I left hoping that my positivity had helped him slightly, although he said little to encourage me to think that might have been the case.

Lakes and fast flowing streams appeared more and more frequently, as did the evidence of beaver-built dams. There were fewer buildings even though I was following a major route, and the gloriously winding bends were safe to ride. The road seemed to be built just for motorcyclists to enjoy on a sunny day, and I had certainly been doing that.

A long day's ride the following morning and afternoon took me effortlessly ever northwards. Larger lakes with mirror-like surfaces produced reflections which defied reality. Near vertical limestone cliffs rose and faded but wedged the road in to narrow gaps between rivers and rail tracks. Every now and then trucks carrying the tools of heavy industry would rumble beside me in one direction of the other. I took this to be signs of oil and gas exploration ahead.

A night in a town which had just had its electricity supply cut off by an industrial accident proved interesting as the only food it had to offer me was from the bakery which had to sell its entire stock before it perished. The baker was a busy man that evening.

A further half day ride took me through an interesting place called Chetwynd which featured a remarkable collection of tree-trunk chainsaw carvings along its main street. The day ended early with a rest at Dawson Creek. This town proudly signposted that I was now entering the World Famous Alaska Highway.

I always had a little chuckle to myself when I saw North Americans refer to 'World Famous' as I had met so many over the years who had little or no idea what happened beyond their shores. This highway was quite probably famous in their world, but not in most people's. Nevertheless I thought it was interesting.

After the attack on Pearl Harbour, Hawaii, in World War Two, the US government funded the construction of the Alaska Highway to channel resources from contiguous USA to its outpost, Alaska. To be more precise it re-constructed rather constructed the highway, improving sections and bridges, as well as shortening connections between small towns. The remarkable fact about the 1700 mile re-construction was that it only took eight months to complete.

It had subsequently been straightened and shortened a few more times to about 1380 miles. I was gripped by its conception, marvelled in its construction, and challenged myself to ride it.

At this point I should have turned around to head east, but it was north gain for me. The road was still good and easy to ride and the scenery was glorious. An extra layer or two of clothing was increasingly necessary, and my wet weather top layer was on and off throughout most days. After a couple of larger towns the traffic thinned to just a few trucks, cars and the odd bike every now and then. However, I was increasingly joined by other road users. Bisons mainly. Several small herds lumbered across the highway. Some a little ahead of me - I always allowed the bulls to cross first - and at other times I would turn a bend and find myself right amongst them. There were also plenty of magnificent looking elks, some caribou and a couple of moose. I managed to spot some black bears too, including four cubs who had just crossed the road and slipped in to some bushes. I stopped to say hello, checked to see if a parent was with them, but rode on, quite rapidly initially, just in case they had spotted me first. Bighorn sheep were native to one particular rocky section and let me know I was in their territory by refusing to move out of the middle of the road.

There was a delightful mix of places named by the indigenous population, and others named by settlers. I stayed the night in Toad River. A dusty collection of thousands of baseball caps covered the ceiling of the highway service centre. I never found out why, but in any case was busy replacing yet another of the bolts holding my luggage set in place. One more had snapped in half, but not one of the two I had replaced in central Bolivia.

Otherwise, things were going well. Within the space of my helmet once more, I had started to develop another idea. This road I was on, The Alaska Highway, would take me to Alaska. Not a difficult conclusion. Nor indeed was the realisation that Alaska was part of the United States. The country that had so far not given me permission to enter. I was so close to it; tantalisingly so. Too tempting not to give it one more go.

I rode right up to the Beaver Creek - Alcan border crossing on the crest of a small hill. It was a building like all other border posts, designed for function not aesthetics. Rectangular and grey, inevitably, with cameras, lights and barriers. I stopped and presented my passport to the officer at the window, and immediately offered an explanation.

"Sir, I know I do not have permission to enter the United States. After leaving London England a year ago to ride my motorcycle around the world, I travelled through Iran and because of that, possibly, I have not yet been given permission to enter your country. It has been hugely disappointing to me, especially as I have been nothing but a friend to the United States for over thirty years of business and vacation visits. I have come here today to ask you to keep hold of my passport for just ten minutes, hoping that you will let me in and put a smile back on my face. Your gesture of goodwill towards me will be very much appreciated."

I wore a cheeky but respectful smile. The U.S. Customs and Border Protection officer responded with a stern poker-face. He left the counter and returned a minute later to ask me to park my bike to the side, and enter his office. Not quite the reaction I had hoped for.

The atmosphere at his intimidatingly high counter was even sterner. His superior officer oversaw the procedure that followed, but never once looked me in the eye. After clearing his throat he explained to me that I was now in the United States, wholly inside it. The beautifully hand carved wooden "Welcome to Alaska" sign, at the edge of a parking lot at the bottom of the hill, was in fact the border. I responded by stating that his office looked very much like the border to me, and that I had not seen any line or indication of any kind to suggest that the border was in the parking lot, a minute back down the hill. He established his authority well at that point, telling me he knew exactly where the border was. I felt the need to apologise for my error, but I am sure he realised that these were no more than words tumbling out of my mouth. After consulting with his superior officer once more, he returned to tell me that I would have to be recorded as an 'undocumented alien'.

Well, that was an interesting turn of events. Flashing through my mind were the stories of others who had ridden around the world before me, and written accounts of their adventure. These included kidnapping, false imprisonment, arrest and detention. I felt sure that every one of those authors would rather not have had to endure such experiences, but it nevertheless had given their publishers headline grabbing opportunities. To date, nothing remotely similar to that had happened to me, and Canada was to be the last country on my tour. The prospect of arrest and a night in a jail, provided it was clean and comfortable, appealed to me. It would have given me something to talk about.

Without much hesitation though, I realised I had better do my best to avoid that. Cowardly, I lowered my head, and apologised again, this time sincerely.

"It had not been my intention to cross your border illegally. I have great respect for the law. I wanted to ask you if you could help put a smile back on my face again, that's all. I have come here today because I love your country, not because I wanted to break into it".

He suggested that I changed my story. I was not keen on that as it would not be the truth. However, his proposed explanation would be a workable solution for the paper trail he would have to record. He suggested I changed it from 'asking to be allowed in for ten minutes', to 'asking if my visa application had been approved'.

I agreed, rode in a u-turn, collected my passport at the window on the other side of his office, and on down the hill. I stopped at the 'Welcome to Canada' message on the back of the 'Welcome to Alaska' message and searched for a white line that might have been the actual border marker that I had missed. There was no white line. I dismounted for a photo and slug of water. It was then, and only then, that I realised there was in fact a smile on my face after all. The one I had sought when I got to the top of the hill an hour earlier. I leapt childishly around the parking lot, whooping and hollering loudly, as a new thought had just occurred to me. If only for an hour, illegally, I had indeed got into the United States of America.

———

The smile stayed with me all the way back down the Alaska Highway. A few places were familiar to me. Fuel stations were always a welcome sight, but for meal breaks and hotels I deliberately chose new experiences. After a couple of days in relative wilderness I stopped at Watson Lake. On the way up I had noticed a colourful exhibit on the side of the road titled 'Sign

Post Forest'. Hundreds of straight evergreen trees, and dozens of additional wooden posts, were all covered in signs. People from all over the world had brought with them a signpost from their hometown, and nailed them to the trees. Many looked liked they might have been municipal property, indicating the name of their home town, perhaps the State too, and population size. Others were distance markers, and some were vehicle licence plates. The more transfixed I became, the more I realised there were quite a few signs which could only have been made at home before journeying to Watson Lake. They had a prefabricated feel to them. One proudly told me that the visitor had travelled there in 1991 from Keighley, West Yorkshire. That happens to be the home town of my favourite English brewer; Timothy Taylor. I took note of it, and licked my lips.

I sought an explanation for the Signpost Forest and found it in the longstanding tradition of 'leaving your mark'. In 1942 a homesick soldier who was working on the construction of the Alaska Highway added his hometown sign to an army mileage post. Others followed, and the forest grew. To me it represented the relationship between a traveller, their journey, and a connection to home.

It took three days continuous riding before I returned to Dawson Creek, where I turned east for the first time. Stopping for a night in Grand Prairie, Alberta, I noticed a hardware store next to my hotel. This oil, gas and agriculture specialist was able to sell me a fresh selection of bolts for my troublesome pannier set. The packet was inscribed '10X hardened for automotive use'. They solved the problem for good.

The following day's first fuel stop drew me in with a promise of fresh cooked doughnuts, indicated by their larger than life sized plastic model of one up the road.
It was well worth stopping not only for doughnuts but also for a conversation. An elderly gentleman had stopped to collect his mail and after admiring my bike, sought me out. He recognised my country sticker and knew something about Triumphs too. In fact many gentlemen of a certain age had stopped me all over the

world to tell me they used to ride a Triumph in the 1960s. They would also tell me that they leaked oil.

This gentleman volunteered more information about himself. He was a Hutterite. One of thousands in fact who lived in remote farming communities in central Canada. Much like the Mennonites of east Bolivia, they had escaped from religious persecution in central Europe centuries earlier. I took his appearance to be typical of men of a similar belief. Oversized denim jeans, held up by braces, over a thick woollen check shirt, with a wide brimmed straw hat. He had a heavy white beard, but with shaved top lip. His brief conversation with me was charming and warm, and made it easy for me to conclude that the love inside him was a reflection of the love he had for his God.

Edmonton was next on my route, home city to Michele who I had met in the centre of Australia on her bus tour around half the world. She was already working hard to save for her next trip from Morocco to South Africa down the west coast of the continent. Her spirit of adventure was unstoppable.

I also met Cynthia Lodgepole. No, I didn't. I made her name up. I rode past a turning for a small town called Cynthia, which also signposted another small town called Lodgepole. I put the two together and imagined them as one. As I have written before, there were strange thoughts circulating inside my helmet as I rode along.

Michele encouraged me to take a slight detour, which had been on my mind for a while anyway. She recommended I rode through Jasper National Park and Banff National Park. On a map, Highway 93 appeared to run in a straight line through both, but in fact it followed the twists and turns of the Bow River and skimmed Lake Louise. This route proved to be the most glorious single day ride of my entire journey. I had marvelled at many landscapes before this, and many beautiful countries offering me many beautiful moments. But from dawn till dusk, this one day ride was the best. It could have been just as enjoyable over several days, or perhaps a week. All in Alberta, it carved its way through the high Rockies. The terrain was mountainous, with numerous glaciers and ice fields, dense coniferous forests and alpine shrubs. The road was generously wide and gloriously rewarding. Numerous view points, trail heads, turnouts and picnic opportunities made this feel well managed but still magnificently wild.

I stopped beside the river in a clearing at the head of a small parking area. This was a perfect spot to take a series of product videos that I had been thinking about for a while. The thoughts were part of a process of conclusions I was trying to come to about my life in the last year and a half. Most of the thoughts were still without conclusion to this point but I decided I could at least try and articulate some of them. The short videos were to all be about the products which had enabled and enhanced my journey beyond question.

The first was an electrical travel adapter by Skross. A friend of mine had given it to me just before I left. It was compact, robust, universally useable, and included two USB outputs. I used it every single night of the trip.

The second was my Water-to-Go bottle. I could fill it up from bathroom taps and fountains as it safely removed 99.9% of the stuff my body would not care to receive, as well as saving me a small fortune because I did not have to buy water. More importantly, it avoided the need for me to dispose of hundreds of plastic bottles. It contained a filter in the top which needed to be replaced every three hundred refills. I was never ill from drinking water.

The third was a Shark Evo helmet which I bought half way around my world in Australia. It was not only comfortable but also extremely versatile. It could be worn as a full face helmet, with or without a clear visor partly or wholly down, with or without a sun visor partly or wholly down, or as an open face helmet with the chin portion fully folded back. A wind deflector under my chin, and ventilation holes in the top also helped ensure my comfort irrespective of temperature, precipitation or speed.

The fourth manufacturer was Apple. A MacBook Pro, iPhone, iPad and iCloud account ensured I had perfect communication, storage and back-up to hand every day.

And finally, there was Triumph Motorcycles. My Rocket X was comfortable, safe, and reliable, attracting the level of attention I sought like no other machine could. Triumph's global service network served me well when I needed them.

For the record, I neither solicited nor received any reward from the manufacturers of these products. Nor indeed from anybody. My trip was entirely self funded.

My day came quite abruptly to an end as I slipped off the mountains on to flat land. The Prairies took over at that point, and were very flat indeed. It would take me two full days to ride them.

22. Fixed.

Wheat, wheat, then more wheat fields filled the landscape. Grain silos and trains pulling one hundred covered hoppers at a time evidenced the commercial activity between them, as well as Highway 1, taking me across Canada. I rode from Calgary in the west, once known as 'Cowtown' as it was the major railhead for historic cattle drives, towards the 'Great Lakes'. Nothing much changed for over a thousand miles, but in itself, that was interesting to me. It took me back to those early geography lessons at school again. The ones that had fuelled my interest in The Taj Mahal, Mount Everest and Uluru. The Canadian Prairies and their ability to grow more wheat than I could possibly imagine, had now enveloped me. Every gentle undulation revealed more and more. Other grains and crops were being grown too, and cattle were everywhere, but it was the wheat that I chose to recall.

--- ---

There was plenty of time for thoughts to circulate inside my helmet again. With not too much longer to go on my journey, of course I started to think of home. It was to be Lyon, not London, but I would head to England first. I was getting anxious about seeing my immediate family again, including Sue's family. I would have to deal with all the negative issues they still had with me as a matter of first priority. I wasn't looking forward to doing so, but recognised it had to be done. There would be relief and tears that I had returned home safely, and tears for Sue too. I had left them in an early stage of grieving, and they had remained at exactly that point in time, so it seemed. I was the focus of their grief, to an extent, and had left them. It was clear to all that my journey had been a tremendous accelerant to the grieving process for me, but not for them. They were still telling me that I had met Dalila too soon. I continued to acknowledge that was the case, trying always to be humble and respectful to them when I responded to their comments. I made no apology for falling in love with her. They had to accept that, and to a certain extent they did so. They held nothing against her. It had happened, and could not be changed. However, they continued to find my behaviour unacceptable. That anger exploded when I announced our marriage and I had been working on calming things down since then. Emails flowing from some family members, not all, had been arriving with ever increasing venom in their tone. They rebuked and assassinated me. My return would give them a further opportunity to explain their feelings to me, and I would have to politely absorb their criticism without responding in the same tone. I remained determined not to fall out with them. I loved them all dearly.

I was also getting desperate to see my close friends again. Unlike my family I had received nothing but love and support from them, without judgement.

During the journey I had met a number of widowers and widows. Men in particular had experienced similar negativity on meeting someone else sooner rather than later. All of the widows I met had not found another man to share their life again, and showed no real sign of wanting to do so. I had also been reading more about this syndrome. It seemed my experience was far from unique.

I returned to the earlier observation that men felt the need to fix their broken lives after their wife had died. This was especially the case after a long and happy marriage, I learnt. It could often be misinterpreted as a lack of love for the departed, but in fact was exactly the opposite. Early in my journey I had tried to explain to myself that as so much love had poured out of me in Sue's direction, it continued to pour out after she had gone, and needed a new home. Dalila had entered my life at that point. I had also discovered that this feeling had been articulated by others before me. My immediate family had shown no consideration in these respects. In fact, they had shown little consideration for my needs at all, only their own. However, I also learnt that dealing with these issues was complex. My behaviour must have felt like something of a betrayal to them, even though everybody realised that at some point, the world would continue to turn. It was just too soon for them. I had not even given them enough time to remember Sue on the first birthday after her death, before meeting Dalila, let alone the first anniversary of her passing.

One opinion offered to me encouraged me to question whether or not my family was in a position to judge when might be 'too soon' for me. It was me, not them, who had suffered the most. However, I was also reminded that there was no timeline for grief. There was no timeline for falling in love again either.

I also heard a ghastly phrase: 'Women mourn, men replace'. There was no room for love in that over-simplification. Love had been the dominant force in my life, and remained so. However, as the women especially in my immediate family were still mourning, I would have to return to England and respect that their mechanism for handling Sue's passing, was different to mine.

― ― ―

The Rocket and I slid easily enough over Alberta, Saskatchewan and Manitoba before entering Ontario. The gentle undulations of the Prairies were replaced by hills, forests, rivers and small lakes. I was tingling with excitement and relishing the thought of my first ever sighting of Lake Superior, but without warning it appeared just over the brow of a rise. All I could see was a small inlet at first, and later a wider shoreline. I knew I was not going to be able to see it all in one vista but was still expecting a bigger view. Perhaps again those early geography lessons had led me to expect something more. It was after all the largest freshwater lake in the world. A day and half later, after solid riding, I realised I had only covered half of its northern shoreline. It was after all, very, very big.

In Lima, Peru I had come across a statue of Paddington Bear. The author Michael Bond had written that his marmalade loving character had come from "deepest, darkest Peru". In White River, Canada I chanced upon another statue of a bear. This one was Winnie the Pooh. To my great surprise and delight I learnt that Winnie had really existed. In 1914 she was bought by a Canadian Army Veterinary Surgeon and taken to England as a war mascot. He named her Winnie after his hometown, Winnipeg. At the end of the First World War he left her in London Zoo, and was eventually admired by author A. A. Milne and his son Christopher. Winnie loved honey.

Riding around Lake Huron took another day and a half. Time enough to firm up plans for the last couple of weeks of my journey. I was heading towards London, on Thames River, the one in Ontario that is. There I met up with Kevin and his daughter Liza. They were amongst the many American friends I had hoped to see in the US, but couldn't. Instead they offered to come and see me in Canada. I was thrilled by their gesture. Although living in Colorado they were visiting family near Lake St. Clair, Michigan, not far across the border. Reminiscing about old times, old friends, and new experiences, we chatted frantically over a long lunch and walk around London. One day was never going to be enough, but I was so grateful to them for the effort and thoughtfulness behind their visit.

The excitingly modern vibrant centre of Toronto was my next stop. Here I caught up with another dear friend from the US. Debbie had flown in from New York City just to see me too. She warmed my heart. I had known Debbie for many years, connected to each other by friends and family. We too had plenty to talk about, but ever the perfect organiser she had treated me to tickets for a major baseball game. Toronto Blue Jays took on Boston Red Sox and, surprisingly as the Red Box were current champions, the Blue Jays won by three points.
Later, we shot up to the glass viewing gallery, with both downward and distant views, at the top of the iconic CN Tower, and marvelled at the distorted perspectives. On our last day, a gloriously sunny one, we took the Hornblower boat trip out to the spray and turbulence under Niagara Falls. Unlike the multiple falls at Iguazu in Argentina, Niagara had just three, with the most notable being Horseshoe Falls. We laughed a great deal in those few days.

In a further rebuttal to my US visa application failure, yet more friends offered to cross over the border from the US to Canada just to see me. Marvin and Susan drove up from New York State and joined me in Montreal for a couple of days. The conversation, as always with Marvin, was intelligent and amusing. He had sneaked in a small bag of soil which we deposited in a hotel back yard and symbolically added a small stars and stripes flag on it, declaring that I had indeed reached US soil.

Dalila's youngest sister, Lhallia, who I had not met the previous Christmas in Lyon with all the other family members, had settled in Montreal. I didn't hesitate to get in touch and introduce myself, enjoying an excellent evening meal together in the process.

— — —

The very final day of my trip arrived with considerable sadness. I delivered my bike to a Montreal airport warehouse for crating, paperwork and so on as usual, and off it went to Motofreight at Heathrow, London.
Following swiftly after that was a visit to a store to buy yet another suitcase. This was the sixth and final time that I had needed to do so. A disadvantage to fitting hard panniers to the bike was that the contents were either loose or in soft bags. Not suitable for flying. I bought, then abandoned in hotel bedrooms, the cheapest case I could find on each occasion that I had slipped off for my non-riding adventures. Arriving in Auckland, New Zealand, the case I bought on Bali had disintegrated spectacularly, losing three of its four wheels, and two of its three handles. In Montreal, I skipped the cheap option in favour of one I hoped to keep for many years to come. By using WhatsApp from the store, Dalila chose the colour.

In England I spent five days rushing around seeing as many family members and friends as I could, and squeezed in brief visits to Triumph Jack Lilley Ashford, The Ace Cafe London and The Bike Shed London. At the Ace I recorded a photo of myself, at later compared it to the one that was taken at the start. I found the difference quite remarkable. A younger man had returned than the one who had left a year and a half earlier. It was clearly visible in my face, smile and body pose.

I arranged to return to The Bike Shed MC a month later to give a talk and slide show to invited friends. The contents had been rehearsed many times inside my helmet in recent months, and was divided into two halves. The first was about the journey and experiences, with an attempt to explain not just what had happened, but why I had done it. The second was all about Dalila, our *rendez-vous* around the world, our love, and our incredible story. At least, we thought it was incredible. My audience included friends who had traveled there from Spain, as well as Elaine who I had met for just one hour on the second day of my trip. Ben, Suzie's brother, was also there - I had caught up with Suzie and her partner Kelvin in Peru. Stephen and Alexandra, who I had met at Uluru and again in Lima took me completely by surprise. They had not told me of their secret plan to travel from their home in Switzerland to be there for my talk. The whole day was extremely emotional.

― ― ―

I could have ridden from London to Lyon in a day. It would have been a long day, and I would have arrived late and tired. Preferring instead to arrive with a generous smile on my face, and savour the moment together, I split the journey into a day and a half. That would also give me more time for some final helmet conversations with myself.

After setting out to deliver two messages to the world, and share some passions, I needed to come to some conclusions about their relative successes. Encouraging people to "ride a motorcycle because it can be so much fun" had been a huge success. Every conversation I had with people proved it, if only because I had ridden all the way to them from London. Their smile was all I needed to see to know with absolute certainty that the message was well received. Some of the longest conversations started with this message. I know that I changed lives too. Contrastingly, the "please stop smoking" message was a failure. Most smokers did not want to hear this, and some even told me that their chosen habit was their business, but not mine. I had tried to link the message to raise some money for Cancer Research UK, in Sue's name, but that goal too achieved little. However, three people later told me they had given up smoking, and cited my message as helpful though not instrumental.

My self-gratifying visits to football stadiums in Barcelona, Madrid, Milan and Rio de Janeiro were highlights for me, but did little to further my idea of sharing my passion for Chelsea Football Club. I had given away most of the fifty badges that I had at the start, but they were not received in a way I had hoped. The club really did not need any help from me at all, and never once reacted to the social media tags I used.

However, sharing my love for Triumph Motorcycles, was very much appreciated by the company. Five times throughout my journey they featured my story in their on-line magazine 'For the Ride'. I was so grateful to them for explaining my motivations and describing my experiences. They handled sensitive issues very well indeed.

Promoting my support for The Ted Simon Foundation proved quite difficult though, as I received blank looks almost every time I mentioned it. However, their desire to help encourage others to venture in to the world, and communicate their understanding of it, was never far from my thoughts.

I travelled as a proud Fellow of the Royal Geographical Society, and talked about their work on quite a few occasions. Their remit, in an extremely abbreviated form, was to 'popularise geography', and in a very small way I managed to communicate that. At the back of my mind was the hope that one day I might be invited to give a lecture to the Society on my journey. It was a naive thought at best, but born from the numerous Monday Night lectures I had attended over the years. Many of the world's most remarkable geographers and high achievers had entertained and educated me with their discourses. Most would start the evening by telling the audience that they felt honoured to have been invited to address the Society President and members. Following in their footsteps would be an honour that I could scarcely conceive. I had not carried out any geographical research, nor unearthed any new phenomenon. I had learnt nothing new to communicate to them and I decided that I should not expect an invitation. Many years beforehand I had listened to a couple give a lecture on their world tour in a classic car. Interesting enough, but little more than a lengthy holiday. I had also listened to Charley Boorman lecture on his long way round. Although I had enjoyed the evening, he received a mixed reaction to his well rehearsed talk. We gave a standing ovation to Alastair Humphreys after he had spent four years cycling around the world. His account was exceptionally entertaining. Anything I could say about my journey would pale by comparison.

Regrettably, and to my surprise, I had not managed to come to any sort of conclusion about how I was going to earn a living after my return. I had set off expecting to uncover exciting opportunities on my journey. New business ideas for example, or new products to stimulate the entrepreneur inside me. I had come across a couple but they didn't interest me enough to do anything but think about them for a while. To be honest, after forty odd years of hard work I had thoroughly enjoyed not working for the last two years. I had been putting more and more thought about not working in the commercial world, and was trying to think outside of the box. Or at least trying to think outside of the box that I had put myself in for so long. No positive conclusion had emerged, but would have to sooner rather than later. I needed money again. I wanted money again. I wanted the best for Dalila and I.

— — —

Iran, India and perhaps Indonesia had finally rid me of misconceptions and prejudices that had lingered over the years. It was all down to cultural differences I realised, and once accepted, I learned to love all countries and their peoples.
Any lingering fears had gone too, probably down to guns and machetes in South America. I thought it probable that some more fears might emerge in time, as the world and I changed, but I would be much better equipped to deal with them.
The effort I was making not to use the word 'hate', was succeeding. Whenever someone used it in my company I would

reply to tell them that I hated nothing. The more I did so, the more I believed it myself.

And so finally I arrived in Lyon, and headed straight for the cafe by Dalila's apartment where we had met sixteen months earlier. She was there with her daughter Marie-Sarah. We all embraced - the family was complete.
We didn't hesitate to start the process of me becoming a frenchman. I had my name put on the letter box, took french language lessons, bought a baguette every day, and had my bike serviced, certified, and converted to a French licence plate - *plaque d'immatriculation*.

--- --- ---

There was one more rather significant task that had to be completed. We still needed to prove to the French government that we had married legally in Mexico.

After Dalila had received back our Marriage Certificate from the Notary in Tulum, with the Apostille stamp added, she presented it to the Town Hall in Lyon, only to be rejected again. I duly sent an electronic copy of my Birth Certificate, as requested, but that too had been rejected. Despite carefully guarding my original Birth Certificate all my life, I was bitterly disappointed. We discovered that a copy could be ordered on line, with a date attached to the order. If I presented that to the Town Hall within three months of that date, it would be accepted. Oh, of course it had to be translated in to French, using only a government approved service, just as we had to do with the Mexican marriage certificate several months back. Eventually, with a huge sigh of relief on our part, the Town Hall accepted all the documents.
However, another step in the process was then, and only then, revealed to us. The entire package of documents would have to go to a Consulate service office somewhere else in France, from where they would be sent back to Mexico again, for authentication. They would take up to six months to complete the process. *Putain!*, as they often say in France.

And then one day, the following spring, the process finally reached its conclusion. France accepted that we were legally married, and my rebirth was complete.

THE END

&

THE BEGINNING

MARK HOLMES

For Dalila

Addendum

5 Continents: Europe, Asia, Australasia, South America, North America.
36 Countries: Northern Ireland (part of the UK but I include it because I had never previously been to it). Ireland. France. Spain. Portugal. Andorra. Italy. Malta. Slovenia. Croatia. Bosnia. Serbia. Montenegro. Albania. Greece. Turkey. Iran. Dubai. India. Nepal. Cambodia. Malaysia. Indonesia. New Zealand. Australia. 26,056 miles / 41,600 kilometres to this point. Chile. Argentina. Brazil. Bolivia. Peru. Mexico. Ecuador. Colombia. Canada. USA.
39,000 miles / 61,000 kilometres.
2 breakdowns. A fuse caused overheating and a split coolant pipe in Jakarta, Indonesia. A spring broke in my gearbox in Rio de Janeiro, Brazil.
0 punctures.
0 drops (the bike)
Cost. Possibly somewhere between £50,000 and £75,000.
190 different beds.
6 nights camping.
152 days riding my Triumph Rocket X, and 14 days riding a hired Triumph Tiger 800.
506 days away from 1st April 2017 to 20th. August 2018.
40 flights
16 ferries
1 wife

Best products taken:
Triumph Rocket X
Apple Mac Book Pro and iPhone
Shark Helmet
Water-to-go bottle
Skross power adapter

Worst products taken:
Back2You motorcycle tracker
White T-shirts

Not used products taken:
Trainers and gym kit
Swiss army knife
Bandages
Condoms

All the other stuff:
A selection of simple hand tools, together with the original bike tool kit.
Bolts, rubber bands, gaffer tape, Rescue Tape, clamps, string, Chelsea FC badges, pens, and note books.
Clear sealable bag with First aid kit including bandages, plasters, scissors, thermometer, anti-malaria tablets, paracetamol, Ibuprofen, Imodium, tiger balm, vaseline, and ankle support.
Clear sealable bag with phone charger, camera battery charger, laptop power supply, electric toothbrush charger, one terabyte Lacie backup, assorted power adapters, head torch, visiting cards, and padlocks.
Assorted paperwork and receipts collected along the journey.
iPad for backup.
Helmet bag with lock.
Chain and padlock.
Hammer.
Assorted cloths.
Small soft backpack.
Tent.
Sleeping bag.
Inflatable mattress.

The contents of the top box was lifted out daily. It contained my camera - Canon 5D, Water-to-go bottle, MacBook Pro, bike registration details with Carnet, and a non-padded clothes bag containing:
Two pairs of jeans.
One pair of linen trousers.
Two long sleeved tops.
Two long sleeved shirts.
Four short sleeved shirts.

Six T-shirts.
Wash bag.
Pants and socks.
Casual jacket.
One pair soft shoes.
One pair sandals.
Spectacles, sun glasses.
Note pad and pen.
Photos of Sue in a small album.
Hand washing powder for clothes.

Leather motorcycle jacket.
Leather motorcycle jeans.
Motorcycle boots.
Neck sock.
Summer gloves.
Intermediate gloves.
Winter gloves, plug-in.
Waterproof jacket.
Waterproof leggings.

Triumph Dealers visited:
Istanbul
Dubai
Mumbai
Delhi
Kuala Lumpur
Jakarta
Brisbane
Sydney
Rio de Janeiro
Lima
Lyon

Favourite Countries visited

I had three favourites for different reasons:
Iran for the hospitality of the people.
India for being the most fascinating.

New Zealand for being the most beautiful single country.

Favourite Cities visited

I had three favourites for different reasons:
Rome for its historic centre and romance.
Sydney for its quality and excitement.
Rio de Janeiro for its rhythm.

Why you need a Carnet to take a vehicle into many countries, and how to get it.

Correct at July 2017.

Before I left the UK on 1st April 2017 I researched, on line, the need to get a Carnet to take my bike into countries beyond the EU. I found, conflicting, contradictory, confusing and largely obsolete information. Feeling the pressure with all the other things I wanted to do before leaving, which mostly included spending as much time as possible with friends and family, I gave up. Many previous motorcycle travellers have told me that at some point you just have to decide to go, ready or not. So that is what I did. Go, but without a Carnet. That proved to be the wrong decision.
My advice to everyone planning a trip, with a vehicle, is to get your Carnet BEFORE you leave your home country.

A Carnet de Passages en Douane is basically a legal promise that permits you to bring a vehicle in to a country, and take it out again within the agreed time. By making this promise you are permitted to not pay that country's import duty and tax. If you fail to honour that promise then there is a stiff price to pay. More on that later.
The Carnet document is multi-part. One page per country; each page is divided in to three. The lower part is for the import process and is retained at the entry border with a reference number, stamp, date and signature. The top left part has the same details, but remains attached to the Carnet document. At the exit border the middle part, bearing the same reference, is retained

and later matched to the import record. It's a simple principle, but most importantly, it is the Carnet holder's responsibility to make sure that the customs process is correctly followed. The top right part of each page is stamped and retained by you. Again, if at the end of the trip there is a rubber stamp or detail missing, then you are liable to the penalty unless you can prove otherwise.

The governing body for countries who accept the Carnet procedure is the Federation International de l' Automobile (FIA). Check out their website for up to date information.

They list the countries who currently require a Carnet. But just look at the first few lines.

"This list may not be up to date due to changes in customs formalities or border procedures. Certain countries may accept the CPD even though they fall outside the AIT/FIA customs documents network. Countries may appear in this list but NOT on the CPD cover, notably those in which there is no AIT/FIA guarantor association. In certain countries of Africa, Asia, the Middle East and Central & South America, the CPD is not officially required, but is sometimes used to facilitate temporary importation."

My big mistake was deciding to ignore this and work it out as I went along. Nearing Turkey's border with Iran I learnt that I would definitely need a Carnet for Iran, but it was too late to get one sent from the UK. That cost me 28 hours and several hundred Euros to resolve. I had to buy a dedicated Iran Carnet at the border. Don't try this: It is official (so the Chief of Police told me), but they don't want to do it this way. My suspicion is that this option will soon be removed.

After Iran I was heading for Dubai where I would again need a Carnet.

In the UK, both major motoring organisations, the AA and RAC, used to be the defacto source for Carnets, but have withdrawn the service. They cite diminishing demand and diminishing return on capital employed. My pre-departure research uncovered that more and more countries are removing the need for a Carnet, preferring deregulation and adhocracy.

That just leaves a company called CARS Europe in the UK.

I am pleased to report that their service is fantastic. With cordial efficiency and a genuine desire to help me out of a tight spot, they completed my application promptly and despatched my Carnet to get to me as I reached Iran's southern port, just in time for my passage to Dubai.

You can buy either a 5, 10 or 25 page Carnet depending on the number of countries you intend to visit, or expect to ask you for a Carnet. That's not too expensive. However, the sting in the tail is the deposit. The system requires the value of your vehicle to be deposited in cash, through CARS. Gulp! If you fail to get the Carnet completed correctly, you risk losing this deposit. Alternatively you can pay an Insurer to deposit that bond for you. That's the expensive part! CARS will tell you more.

My Carnet de Passage En Douane was needed in:
Iran
U.A.E.
India
Indonesia
Australia
Argentina

Recipe for home-made lemonade

Serves four.
Start with four fresh lemons, as fresh as can possibly find. Not always easy away from the Tropics, but do your best.
They must be ripe too, but if they are not fresh then don't wait too long for them to ripen.
Cut them in half, and squeeze them well into a bowl. Keep any pulp that falls out, but spoon out any pips and discard them.
For sugar, use four tablespoonfuls of raw cane sugar. In a saucepan of two litres of fresh filtered water, add the sugar and heat gently until all the sugar has dissolved. Store in a fridge until chilled.

Add the lemon juice to the sweetened water and stir well.
Serve in a jug with a sprig of fresh mint, not too much, and a handful of ice cubes, also made from fresh filtered water.
That's it. Enjoy!

REBIRTH

" When life gives you lemons, make lemonade".

The phrase has been largely attributed to Dale Carnegie in his 1948 book, "How to stop worrying and start living": 'If you have a lemon, make lemonade". However, it was author Elbert Hubbard who first used it in an obituary to a dwarf actor friend. "He picked up the lemons that fate had sent him and started a lemonade-stand."

Printed in Poland
by Amazon Fulfillment
Poland Sp. z o.o., Wrocław